4·50

Counselling
in a Troubled Society

COUNSELLING
in a Troubled Society

by

HARRY AND MARGARET DEAN

Quartermaine House Ltd.
Windmill Road, Sunbury, Middx., U.K.
1981

First published by Quartermaine House Ltd. 1981
© Harry and Margaret Dean
ISBN 0 905898 13 3

Acknowledgements

The authors wish to acknowledge and give special thanks to the following for permission to use quotations as referenced in the text:

A.D. Peters & Co. Ltd., London; Associated Book Publishers Ltd., London; Souvenir Press Ltd., London; Abingdon Press, Nashville, U.S.A.; Jonathan Cape Ltd., London; Estate of Hermann Hesse; John Calder (Publishers) Ltd., London; CRAC (Careers Research & Advisory Centre, Cambridge; Tavistock Publications Ltd., London; National Marriage Guidance Council Pubs., Bristol; Brooks/Cole Publishing Co., California, U.S.A.; George Allen & Unwin, Hemel Hempstead, Herts.; Sheldon Press, London; W.H. Smith Publishers Inc., New York, U.S.A.; Mayflower Books Inc.; Penguin Books Ltd., London; Fontana Paperbacks, London; T. Shand Publications Ltd., London; Bedford Square Press, London; National Council of Social Service, London; Hodder & Stoughton Ltd., Sevenoaks, Kent.

Printed in Great Britain
by Unwin Brothers Limited
The Gresham Press, Old Woking, Surrey

CONTENTS

To our sons — Elton and Hartley

INTRODUCTION

In Britain counselling is very largely a phenomenon of the past fifteen to twenty years. In the United States its brief history goes back somewhat further.

Ever since time began men have talked over their problems and personal concerns with relatives, friends and acquaintances, but during recent decades counselling has come to be recognised and accepted as a more formalised type of service, with its own fairly well-defined principles and methods of procedure.

In social work the emphasis used to be on practical help, but now social workers do a considerable amount of counselling. There has been development and a growing sense of social responsibility. It is now recognised that an individual's well-being should be the concern of society as a whole. In most developed countries the physical health of citizens is fairly well cared for by a whole range of health services. Counselling seeks to cater for the emotional health of the individual, and society cannot opt out of its responsibility in this important field.

People need to feel secure within themselves if they are to cope with the many difficulties that come their way. Even the normal business of living when there are no complications is too much for some. The disease of 'copelessness' is alarmingly widespread.

This is a disturbed and disturbing age. It seems that there are those in every generation who imagine their own age is the worst there has ever been. Many today have come to this conclusion and tend, therefore, to despair of any possible improvement. Any change, they imagine, must be for the worse.

Such a pessimistic assessment seems to the authors of this book to be unnecessarily wide of the mark and reveals either an ignorance of history or the tendency to be selective when thinking about the past. It is unlikely that this age is appreciably worse than its predecessors. All that can be said with certainty is that it has its own particular tensions and problems.

It is natural and right that we should be concerned about the prevalence of violence in today's world, but we are prone to exaggerate even this when comparing it with the past. In spite of hooliganism and muggings, it is still safer to walk the streets of our big cities today than in any previous century.

For example, in the east end of London throughout the nineteenth century murder was so frequent that the newspapers did not even bother to report it. The famous Jack the Ripper had to murder a second time before any mention was made of him, and even then it was because of the way in which he mutilated his victims. Colin Wilson estimates that a hundred years ago the district of Whitechapel alone could probably have equalled our present national average for murders.

These comments are not made in order to encourage complacency, but to help us to see things in perspective. But there are new factors that call for scrutiny.

So let us conclude this introduction and commence the study by asking a number of important questions:

What makes this day and age different from the past?

What features of today's world threaten the peace of mind and emotional stability of the individual?

In what ways does counselling contribute to a person's well-being?

These are some of the basic problems this book seeks to elucidate.

1 The Contemporary Scene

There was a time when the lives of people were so enmeshed in work and the existing social structures that few seemed to have problems of intimacy, identity and security. We appear to be paying a heavy price for our present-day pre-occupation with individualism.

Few would wish to return to the feudal society of the past, but the serf was never in any quandary as to his role in life. He was the farmer, the soldier, or the miller on the feudal estate, and his wife nurtured the next generation as well as bearing her share of the work-load. Even in more recent times sons of farmers, miners and fishermen were expected automatically to follow in father's footsteps.

In those more distant days all group life supported the process that gave individuals their values and, in addition, gave meaning to their lives. Art, literature and religion were the unquestioned sources of value. The great cathedrals were also centres of education, places for acting out the ceremonies that gave meaning to the life of the community, and so to the individual within it. There was little struggle to find meaning, for the meaning was something given. It was there implicit and unquestioned.

In those days the family and social structure were less important than the all-embracing system. With the breakdown of those feudal patterns, however, and the emergence of different economic and social structures, the family became more central in people's lives and had to serve a new purpose. The individual farm or the family-centred craft developed and, as a consequence, a competitive element began to challenge and even to oust the earlier spirit of co-operation. Comparison and contrast took the place of sharing. As the uniqueness of individual families developed their particular traditions, relationships *between* families inevitably became problematical. The cohesiveness of the former structure had gone for ever.

Both romantic and mercenary concepts began to emerge. Individuals started to look for personal happiness and fulfilment, and families sought beneficial marriages that would enhance their status and prestige.

During the nineteenth century the family structure held together reasonably well. Apart from the fast-growing industrial centres, in the small towns and still smaller villages people worked, played, learned and worshipped together. The extended family was still a reality. There was a basic cohesiveness about life. Even so, insecurity in all its forms was on its way.

Our twentieth century has seen major changes in the structure and function of the family. The great migration from the rural areas to the large conurbations of towns and cities has led to the practical extinction of the extended family. We now find ourselves with the nuclear family of father, mother and 1.9 children. Houses and flats are getting smaller but there must be a garage to hold the car that will take the family away from the home on the slightest pretext.

In his excellent book *The Secular City*, Harvey Cox[1] has highlighted the possible gains that urban life provides. We can escape into anonymity if we so desire, and we can actually choose our friends instead of having them thrust upon us. Furthermore, our increasing mobility can enable us to get well away from everything and everyone when we wish to escape.

But can the nuclear family meet the emotional and relationship needs of the children growing up in it? Do not they need to relate to the generation beyond that of their parents? In some communities this is coming to be recognised, for there are places where parents can engage not only baby-sitters so that they can have an evening out together, but grannies, so that their children can learn something about the older generation.

When both parents work, as is increasingly the case, the major investment of time, energy and interest outside the home can mean that the home comes to mean less and less. Tired parents may be tempted to retreat from relationships when their children move towards them, and from responsibilities when quite proper demands are being made upon them. It is very often the case that each family member is pursuing some activity away from the home at the same time. This is admirable if the diversity is then brought together and shared, but if different interests mean separate lives the loss of family intimacy can create a wall of loneliness that sooner or later leaves the individual at a loss.

The present-day prevalence of divorce leads to the conclusion that the nuclear family can breed tension and conflict. The question arises, can it meet our basic needs for intimacy, security and identity?

In deploring the public violence on football terraces and the back streets of our cities after dark, the fact needs to be faced that most violence takes place *within the family*. Most murders are crimes of passion committed by people who are related or closely identified in life. Most physical assaults also take place within the family. In every 'civilised' country parents attack their children. In England alone, most weeks, two babies or small children are killed by their parents. The police dread the frequent calls to quell family violence for they are likely themselves to come under attack.

In the United States of America sixty to seventy percent of all couples have used physical violence at least once in their marriage, and in twenty-five percent it has been a recurring pattern. The family unit that ideally should instil an example of intimacy and love may frequently serve as a breeding ground for alienation, violence and cruelty.

Dr. Edgar Jackson writes:

The family that has been emerging from major migrations and economic needs does not seem to be the family that develops real identity, supports true intimacy and provides the surroundings for security in life.[2]

The changing family structure can perhaps be seen most clearly in what is happening to its aged members. Because of advances in medical science more people are living longer, but the multi-generation family is largely a thing of the past. This means that a growing proportion of the elderly find themselves living in retirement homes, groups of flats especially built to house them, or worse than either of these alternatives, in the geriatric wards of large hospitals. A consequence of this is a great deal of loneliness and resentment on the part of some of the old people involved, accompanied by many guilt feelings among their now middle-aged sons and daughters.

In *Who shall live?*, Victor Fuchs[3] contrasts the death rates in the American States of Nevada and Utah. During the period studied Nevada had high educational standards, good health cover, a low level population density and a high income rate. Yet it had the highest death-rate for whites in the U.S.A.

Utah, its next door neighbour, on the other hand, had one of the lowest death-rates. In addition to this, the number of divorced, separated and bereft people in Utah was about half that in Nevada. What was it that made the difference? Victor Fuchs highlights the following facts: In Utah people are more religious; they smoke and drink less; their family life has a greater stability; and, whereas nine out of every ten of Nevada's residents were born elsewhere, the vast majority of Utah's citizens were born in their home state.

It seems that the western world may be in danger of overlooking the fact that a crucial element making for well-being is the ability to live together, to make and sustain worthwhile human relationships. It is certain that loneliness and isolation can break a person's spirit, and it is not surprising that recent years have seen many and varied attempts to establish communes of different sizes and organisation, where openness and sharing are the order of the day.

If these attempts are made for purely selfish reasons, in which people simply use each other, they are bound to fail. But where there is a genuine desire to relate to other people with mutual appreciation, this can lead to shared growth. We need to see ourselves with some clarity. Those who do may very well discover that intimacy, identity and security are the by-products of commitment, of what has been called 'a sense of the cosmos'.

The state of Israel makes much of its kibbutzim in which children are brought up by the community but with parental influence still operating. Claims are made that this pattern eliminates, to all intents and purposes, juvenile crime and hooliganism.

It has certainly been the experience of the developing African countries that the appeal of the city has drawn young people from the tribal areas — where they were known and where exists a strong sense of community — and this has created many problems because of the increase of violence and crime. It does seem that many young people do need the restraints that they most strongly resent.

This study will focus, in the main, on the western situation, but we do well to remind ourselves that it is not only goods that are exported to the third world. We also export all the problems arising out of industrialisation and urbanisation.

THE IMPACT OF SOCIETY

We are social creatures. Our individuality is precious to us, but we do not exist as separate units in society.

Our long dependent childhood ensures that we cannot live without others. There is no such animal as a self-made man or a completely independent individual. A baby becomes a person only through contact with others. It has been said that we all lay like idiots in the cradle until others smiled us into smiling back and talked us into talking. Society is necessary to us.

We need others if our deep needs of being liked and loved are to be met. Humans need love, not simply during their early years — although these are the most important because everyone is at his most vulnerable then — but throughout the whole of life. We need the interest and interaction of others in order to be ourselves.

Harold, (all names used for illustrative purposes throughout this book are fictional) a young man of great distinction and qualities, in his mid-twenties, was lost for three days and nights in the Norwegian snows. For over seventy hours he lived in a completely white world against the background of a totally undifferentiated environment. He found himself losing touch with his own reality. As a person he began to disintegrate. Who was he? What was he? Where was he?
Eventually another figure came out of that white world and spoke his name. 'Are you Harold . . .?' came the vital question. Harold's relief lay not so much in the realisation that his life was spared, but in hearing someone addressing him by name. Because someone else knew he existed, he could continue to believe in his own existence.

We become what we are addressed. We begin life by living up to others' expectations of us and, unless something happens to make us question this process, we can go through the whole of life simply responding to the personal and impersonal elements in our environment.

Hence the importance of roles in any given society. They tell an individual what is expected of him and what he can expect from others. This is even true of sexual roles. In her intriguing book *Male and Female*, Margaret Mead[4] shows that our norms of male and female are very largely culturally imposed, in that the generally expected dominance of the male and the submissiveness of the female is reversed in some societies. The full consequences of the women's liberation movement is still to be seen. From our earliest days we learned to play particular roles, and this role-playing not only expressed the feelings and attitudes of a situation, but helped to create them. Children find their sexual identity by playing the expected male and female roles.

The interaction between the developing child and his environment in the long run establishes a sense of personal identity, and this is confirmed as other people recognise it in us. The child who is fully and happily accepted within the family will be able to function with reasonable confidence as he moves out into the wider world.

Many occupations provide a code of conduct that must be obeyed and a role that must be played. We think of doctors, nurses, lawyers, clergy etc. A working-class child moving into middle-class circles may find himself in difficulties. He may be forced to play two roles, one at home and another when away from home. Class differences may not be so pronounced as previously, but they are still with us. We have a deep need to feel ourselves accepted by the group in which we find ourselves, and this may put on us great pressures of which we can be unconscious.

Sula Wolff refers to the differing child-rearing practices in families from different social classes, and how their differences become reflected in the behaviour of the children who tend to develop the personality characteristics of their parents. Citing an American survey of the child-rearing method of almost four hundred mothers, and of the nursery-school behaviour of their five year old children, she writes:

> Working class mothers were generally found to be more indulgent during infancy, offering bottle and dummy more freely than middle class parents. By the time their children were five years old, however, these working class mothers were less openly demonstrative of affection, more often overtly rejecting and stricter about sexual behaviour, table manners and orderliness than middle class mothers. Their children were observed to be more dependent on adults than the middle class children. While working class mothers tolerated aggression in their offspring, they also tended to use physical punishment readily. Working class mothers in fact used concrete rewards and punishments; middle class parents used withdrawal of love as a training method.[5]

When considering the impact of society upon the individual, reference must be made to the undoubted power of the mass media, which can hardly be exaggerated. So much of the thinking of the viewer of television, the listener to the radio, the reader of the world's press, the buyer of glossy magazines, is bound to be influenced, albeit unconsciously. Sooner or later thinking becomes translated into behaviour.

Television in particular can introduce people to new areas of life and encourage changes in behaviour patterns. Consciously or unconsciously viewers may be picking up clues on how to behave in situations and circumstances other than those in which they have personal experience, and this may encourage them to move out beyond their normal environment and, in consequence, find within themselves a new potential.

One of the effects of television is to widen and extend interest in all manner of pursuits. This is particularly true of sports. The fear that television will turn us into a nation of spectators is countered by the fact that more people are participating in sports than ever. This is especially the case in what used to be regarded as minority sports. So, gradually, all kinds of changes are taking place in people's lives.

The fear that television will turn us into a nation of illiterates does not seem to be well-founded either. A television serial is invariably followed by the republication of the book or books on which it is based, and the sales are then phenomenal. All the time viewers are being introduced to authors whose names they would otherwise never have known.

Some sociologists complain that most psychologists, psychoanalysts, psycho-therapists and now counsellors are too individualistic in their approach to people, ignoring the importance of the societal aspects of an individual's life. It is true that most counselling relationships are of a one-to-one character, but counsellors cannot help being aware of the extent to which their clients are the product of social factors. This involves probing into various aspects of the individual client's past life — the family situation, including the client's position in the family; where he has lived and the reason for any changes in location; what educational establishments he has attended; the expectations with which he grew up. Has he climbed up or slidden down the social scale? To what extent has his social background affected his ability to function in adult life. The counsellor knows full well that the social realities can never be ignored.

There is also the interesting fact that much one-to-one counselling is now being supplanted by group work of many kinds. Individual therapy often reveals the need for group therapy. We began life in the one-to-one relationship with our mothers, but then had to move out to include fathers, other family members in an ever-widening circle.

So to the question as to where our identity, our meaning, our personal history and even our humanity come from, we have to say, 'Very largely from the society into which we were born and in which we have lived.' Hence the importance of keeping society under constant surveillance. In a sense it is revealing that totalitarian societies have always had to resort to imprisonment, even to torture, in an attempt to control and silence the dissidents in their midst. It is clear that some individuals have sufficient resilience, courage and conviction to face and resist the most systematic and overwhelming pressures to turn them into automata.

We now know that the person least likely to be able to stand out against totalitarian pressure is the one who has no capacity for being alone; who would, in fact, disintegrate if he were not held together within a group.

Moral Man and Immoral Society is the title of an influential book written by Reinhold Niebuhr. The title reminds us that a society can easily become less moral than the individuals forming it. We will be looking at some of the problematic elements in today's world during the course of this chapter. Here it is interesting to note how Karl Marx saw money as the great enemy of our humanity. Money is the embodiment of exchange value, and seems to threaten man's true being. The machine, which is the embodiment and symbol of our industrial society, creates only dead, inauthentic things. Keep on creating dead things and it is likely to have a deadening effect. This is being felt increasingly to be what is actually happening, and our private life within the family is seen as constituting a shelter for the intimate and authentic, a 'haven in a heartless world'. But this retreat into privacy is no final answer. It can lead to a decline in sociability, the disappearance of the neighbour and of the wider circle of relationships and the lessening of friendship ties, all helping to give further impetus to the modern phenomenon of loneliness.

We need a private space in life, and the desire to be socially acceptable at all costs is to be deplored. An appreciation of the importance of society does not mean that we become total conformists. In Arthur Miller's play, *Death of a Salesman*, Willy Loman represents many of our contemporaries. From selling things he ends up by selling himself and is punished because he submits himself to the society where the 'exchange value' reigns supreme. In reading or watching Miller's play we feel deep down that life should not be like that. We also need the conviction that it can be otherwise.

Society is necessary to us, but so is a critique of society. Without this we may be tyrannised and destroyed by it.

STRUCTURES AND PERSONS

As persons we move all the time from one structured situation to another, and mostly remain unaware of the impact of the structures that seem to be essential to our existence.

It is true we cannot live without structures. We are born into the family structure, move out of the family into a whole series of educational structures, and eventually find ourselves in various work structures as we then establish a new family structure of our own.

George was born a month after his father's death. Both parents — who already had one son — wanted a fair-haired daughter to complete the family of four. With the loss of her husband, the mother was all the more anxious that the coming child should not be another son. Red-haired George, simply by being himself, had let his parents down.

He was dressed as a girl until he was five, and developed into a clumsy, fat lad with no interest in sport. Seeing he was going to grow up male(!) his mother decided on a military career for him. School after school tried to turn him into the 'sporty' type, with army or air-force in mind. Eventually college took over the impossible task. George became a depressed adult. Doctors filled him with drugs. Hospitals gave him electro-convulsive therapy. The unhappy years passed.

George had reached his fifties before a sympathetic psychotherapist helped him to find out who he was and what he really wanted out of life. He had been almost destroyed by institutions (family, school, college, hospital) designed for helping.

What are we to make of this story? It points to the fact that everyone needs an atmosphere in which to grow as a person. Perhaps we can flourish only with others who want to flourish in a similar way.

Someone has said of organisations, 'If I cannot say what I think, my needs cannot be met within that organisation.' Whenever we feel restricted certain questions demand an answer: Is this curtailment of my freedom necessary? Is it right? Can I accept it happily? Is it a liberating constraint? We all need discipline, but this should increasingly come from within ourselves — self-discipline. Whatever structures exist need to be consciously and willingly accepted. To be frightened into obedience makes us less than human.

We all need wide areas of personal freedom in order to grow. We need human contacts where the structures of officialdom can be set aside; where we are free to tell others how it feels to be ourselves in relation to them.

In order to feel fulfilled as human beings we have to be forever pushing out the boundaries, always increasing the area of personal freedom. It is in this task that counselling has an important part to play.

THE AGE OF THE MACHINE

It is necessary to try to assess the impact that modern technology can have on people. In *Justice in Industry*, Peter Mayhew[6] tells of a manager who said, 'Human beings are our most important piece of machinery — like machines, if you don't keep them running, men will go rusty.' Because of this managers are expected 'to acquaint themselves with a new technical literature — on the psycho-sociology of work'.

This is a disturbing, even frightening attitude. When people are actually thought of in terms of machines that must not be allowed to 'go rusty', a process of depersonalisation is already well advanced.

Many will deny that this kind of management thinking is widespread, and that there is an increasing emphasis on the need for more human contacts between 'both sides' of industry, all evidence of this must be welcomed, but much of this newer thinking has yet to be put into operation. Many researchers in the field of industrial relationships discover that managers and workers contrive to be involved with each other only to a minimal extent. The fact that the term 'both sides' is used indicates something of the distance to be bridged.

It seems almost inevitable that the increasing use of the computer will have serious side effects. The computer is with us to stay, and no one will dispute that it is a useful tool for solving certain problems. But it also creates problems. The computer has a mind of sorts, but no emotions. It has to treat people as numbers, and in so doing will contribute to the outmoding of truly personal relationships, and the actual errors it makes can create untold human distress. It is becoming customary to 'blame the computer'.

Industry will have to take steps to counter the depersonalising effects it has on people. Persons are not machines and are more important than machines. Through the computer orders can be given to a machine and the machine is not harmed in the process. But simply to issue orders to a person is, in the long run, detrimental to his personhood. It is now being recognised that some strikes have little to do with the worker's wage-packet, but are a bursting safety-valve indicating that some people are trapped in an unhealthy work-situation.

In *Beyond Contract: Work, Power and Trust Relations*, Alan Fox[7] writes of 'the low discretion syndrome' and of 'low discretion roles'. Any worker who knows he is not regarded as trustworthy, in need of constant supervision, allowed no scope for initiative, is bound to become demoralised. Not being trusted, he does not trust others. This breeds suspicion, and any sense of community withers away.

It has to be admitted that in large sections of industry there is little sense of the enterprise being one of partnership. Because of this, every resolution of a dispute is seen as temporary, a truce before another period of hostility. The 'us and them' attitude makes for a relationship of deceit and bluff *on both sides*, each negotiation starting from unrealistic positions and becoming a war of nerves, neither side being quite sure how far the other can be safely pushed. Brinkmanship becomes a way of life — or death.

The concept of partnership based on justice is the only hope for industrial peace and the building of the desperately needed trust relationships. In the meantime it is not surprising that many find themselves insecure, vaguely if not directly threatened, feeling that things are 'out of joint'.

Alongside all this there is the matter of size. If 'small is beautiful' it follows that 'big is ugly'. The bigger a unit — and this warning applies to educational establishments as well as industrial plants — the hollower it is likely to be, and the more brutal its impact on the individual.

Technology is with us to stay, and no one is going to destroy the computer, but cybernetics is not going to solve the problems related to our complex humanity. Ethel Venables writes:

Measurement is meaningless unless applied to the appropriate data and the most important data about people are not their vital statistics but those relating to their hopes and fears, love and hates, satisfactions and frustrations and to companionship and loneliness. These, together with the mastery of a language in which to discuss them, are the essentially human attributes which distinguish us from the rest of the animal kingdom.[8]

Man needs to realise that to hold a mechanistic view of his own life is both damaging and diminishing. Our personalities are physically based, but our thoughts and feelings are not simply the result of our physiological make-up. If this were the case there would be no point in discussing, or even thinking. The whole world of truth and knowledge would be reduced to complete nonsense, including the mechanistic theory itself for that, too, would have no validity.

Learning to live with technology is not going to get any easier. Sir Linton Andrews, one-time editor of *The Yorkshire Post*, once said: 'In my boyhood the streets of London smelt like a stable: now they smell like a garage. I much prefer a horsey to a horse-power smell'.

Many will echo that sentiment, but will need to concentrate on lessening the garage smells of our towns and cities. At the same time, John Ruskin's words should be borne in mind: 'The degradation of the worker into a machine makes all improvements in material conditions equally vain.'

THIS 'GET' AGE

There are cultures that stress 'doing', others that stress 'being'. Protestantism is linked with the 'work ethic' and the rise of capitalism. 'Doing' leads to 'having', to the importance of possessions, to keeping up with the Jones's, and is in the main typical of the western and northern parts of the world.

Cultures of the eastern and southern parts have traditionally emphasised 'being' rather than 'doing'. The mysticism of the east has always appealed to minorities in the west, where contemplative groups exist as a living protest to frenzied activity and the philosophy of 'grab'. Lao Tse's dictum, 'The way to do is to be' will always have an immediate appeal to some, as does Master Eckhart's statement, 'People should not consider so much what they are to *do*, as what they *are*'. But such attitudes *can* produce lethargy and sloth.

In the Middle East during recent decades there has been an interesting contrast between the driving dynamism of the state of Israel transforming the barrenness of its part of Palestine, and the cheek-by-jowl country of Jordan. Moving from the former into the latter can seem like walking back one to two thousand years (except for the tourists' taxis and the ubiquitous transistor radio).

At this point in world history, it seems that the 'doing' and 'having' cultures intend to change the 'being' cultures into their own image. There is certainly cause here for great concern. Every sensible person desires a unified world, but the thought of a uniform world is demoralising.

A basic argument of this book is emphasised in Lao Tse's dictum, 'The way to *do* is to *be*'. We are too much concerned with the verbs 'to want' (craving), 'to have' (clutching) and 'to do' (fussing). Because these are the operative words in all areas of life — material, political, social, emotional, intellectual, religious — many people are kept in perpetual unrest.

Perhaps one of our fundamental needs is the insight that these three verbs
have significance only in so far as they are included in and transcended by the
verb 'to be'. We need to scrutinise what it is we crave for, clutch at, and fuss
about, all the time asking to what extent they have anything to do with 'being'.
We are human '*beings*', centres of dignity, worth, reality, of 'being'. We can so
easily lose ourselves without being aware of the fact.

When we listen to today's advertisers it seems that no one has enough. This,
that and the other are absolutely essential to our happiness, efficiency, status.
Enough has been defined as 'a little more than you now have'. No one would
argue that there is any inherent goodness in poverty, but prosperity can be
equally, and even more disastrous.

This is no argument for living in the twentieth century as though we are still
in the thirteenth, lighting our homes with candles, washing our clothes in the
nearby stream or cooking our food over an open fire. Electricity, washing
machines, and the latest range are good things to have and use, but they are only
means to life, not the 'be all' and 'end all'. Pride in possessions is a very subtle
thing. We can find ourselves valuing them more than our friendships. Things
are made for use: people are made for love. Sad it is if we love things and use
people.

Isabel Robertson wrote a poem entitled *Materialism*:

> With what an awkward dignity,
> Lacking all spontaneity
> And natural grace, they live
> Who, burdened by possessions move
> Like the raucous peacock
> That carries the bright burden of its tail
> As a dazzling liability,
> And cannot use the asset of the air.

We are earthly creatures, but should not be earthbound.

In connection with the publication of his book *To Have or to Be?*, Erich
Fromm[9] when interviewed by Robert Robinson on BBC Television, said:

> . . . . if my sense of identity is based on what I have, on my possessions; if I
> can say I am what I have, then the question arises 'What am I if I lose what
> I have?' Therefore a sense of identity based on what I have is always
> threatened. A person is anxiously concerned not to lose what he has, because
> he doesn't just lose what he has, he loses his sense of self. If I feel I am what
> I have, and I have nothing any more, then *I* am not, and that sense of identity
> which is based on 'to be' is entirely different, because that can never be taken
> away from me.

In the context of Shakespeare's play, Hamlet's question 'To be or not to be'
has to do with physical suicide, but everyone needs to ask the question of himself
regarding his own inner reality. We can opt out of 'being' while still very much
alive. We may not know we have done so, and others may be equally deceived.
Charles Lamb once said that he'd been dead for years but no one had noticed
it.

There is a difference between our 'being' and the image we show to the world. The inner self, our character structure, the true motivation of our behaviour — these constitute our 'being'. Our external behaviour may partly reflect this, but we often mask part of the truth about ourselves. Kierkegaard, that authority on human despair, once said, 'All despair is fundamentally despair of being ourselves'. If this is so, we must find a way of being ourselves *without despair*.

OUR CHANGING WORLD

It is possibly true that more radical changes have occurred during the present century than in any preceding century, and during the second half the rate of change has undoubtedly been escalating. Now, most people find rapid changes somewhat threatening. Whatever an individual's political views, a built-in conservatism is very wide-spread. Most of us have a vested interest in the *status quo*, so that the prospect of too much change in too short a time-span elicits feelings of anxiety if not panic.

Alvin Toffler[10] in his lively, best-selling book, *Future Shock*, argues that we must come to terms with what he calls 'transience'. There is a new feeling of temporariness in the everyday life of everyday people. This concept can be defined as the rate at which our relationships with things, places, people and information turn over.

Regarding things. This is the throw-away society. Every home is a massive processing machine through which objects flow. Less and less are things made to last. Permanence is an outmoded concept. Built-in obsolescence — relating, for example, to light bulbs, shoes, tights, and even cars — is a fact of life.

Regarding places. People travel faster, further and more frequently than in any previous age. Large sections of every western nation are increasingly mobile, moving — if not from town to town — from one house to another every five to ten years. This means fewer people have roots in a settled community, and the frequency with which many move from place to place breeds what has been called 'loss of commitment'. A man, and his family, on the move is not over-concerned at what is happening to the community he plans to leave the year after next. This withdrawal from participation in the life of a locality cannot but be to the detriment of community life. 'Can an individual or a community survive in any meaningful way without commitment?' is a pertinent question many of today's nomads should be asking.

Regarding people. 'Transience' in relation to places must lead to superficial, passing, limited personal relationships. Friendships hardly become established before they have to be abandoned. 'We'll be in touch', 'See you', we say. But this proves too difficult. We not only leave places, we leave people behind us. Collecting more and more acquaintances we are left with fewer and fewer friends. Friendship demands time, attention, commitment — and these are in short supply.

Regarding information. Toffler states: 'By the time the child born today graduates from university, the amount of knowledge will be four times as great'. The sheer accumulation of information can have an overwhelming and baffling effect on us. No one person can encompass even a smattering of universal knowledge. In order to survive at all the individual may need to specialise, knowing much more about much less.

You may feel that much of the above consists of generalisations; yet, though any particular reader's life may not have been affected by all these aspects, there is enough truth here to 'give us pause'.

There is also the feeling that the moral standards of, say, the pre-war period have undergone considerable change. This has been called the 'permissive society' and permissiveness has been welcomed by many and deplored by some. Certain groups have been pushing for more freedom, others have been fighting rearguard actions to hold back the ever increasing tide of licentiousness.

Few indeed would wish to return to the very doubtful morality of the Victorian era, the hypocrisies of which were a cover for the iniquities equal to any of today's excesses. But already there are many who see quite clearly that unbridled license is not the same as liberty, that personal freedom needs restraints and standards.

In his book *Sexual Suicide*, George Gilder wrote:

Nothing is free, least of all sex, which is bound to our deepest sources of energy, identity and emotion.
Sex can be cheapened, of course, but then, inevitably, it becomes extremely costly to the society as a whole.[11]

Many young people are learning that a rich personal relationship cannot be created by simply engaging in a biological act. Living together without obligation so that either can leave at will, can create as many emotional problems, and lead to as much heartbreak and tragedy as can the 'conventional' marriage relationship. Living without commitment can result in great anxiety. Limited self-giving creates all kinds of threatening uncertainty. Life does not thrive on tentativeness, but becomes a form of unresolved loneliness. Increasingly we are learning that personal identity involves identification and commitment.

Another aspect of change in many western nations is that religious pluralism is now a fact of life. Prior to World War Two, Britain, for example, was recognisably a 'Christian' country. Not that everyone — nor even a majority — went to church. But everyone knew of the strong alliance between church and state. Even if Christian prayers were not said daily within most families, the children were encouraged to say them before going to bed at night. The statute insisting on daily prayers and the regular teaching of the Christian faith was observed in all state schools. We were a Christian nation.

On missionary Sundays, those children who did attend Sunday school were told of the 'heathen' who worshipped gods of wood, stone or metal. There was a whole range of religious isms — Hinduism, Buddhism, Mohammedenism, etc. But all this related to a far distant world, having no bearing on our lives.

Now all is changed. Every world religion is here in our midst. Even if we call all British children 'Christian', in many of our schools there are more non-Christian than Christian. In the 1920s and 1930s citizens in Britain had a simple choice. They could be either Christian or nothing at all. Now they can choose to be Buddhists, Sikhs, Muslim, etc., if they so desire. This religious pluralism makes for complications and can create all kinds of uncertainty. The straightforwardness of much of life has been lost for ever.

The above facts — and many more besides — are anxiety-making and can lead to breakdown. There are many disturbing aspects in our current situation: the widespread misuse of drugs; the prevalence of alcoholism; the politics of nihilism; the sick apathy of millions, old and young alike — to name but a few.

Affluence makes it possible for large numbers of people to withdraw emotionally from the real issues of life. Many withdraw part-time by retreating regularly into the world of televised fantasy, or taking some other periodic escape route. For other 'drop-outs' withdrawal is full-time and total. One young man was very pleased at being called a 'drop-out'. 'It's better than being nothing', he said.

Man's basic problem is to find out who he is, and then to become it. Plants and animals fulfil an inborn destiny — a cat is not a dog; a dog is not a rose; a rose is not a potato. There is no possibility that an elephant will ever change into a bird. In the realm of nature there is a basic constitution so that any potential growth and development is all one unified reality. Not so with man. There are obviously many ways in which we are linked with the animals, but the differences are so fundamental as to put us in an altogether different category. Man has to find himself, to learn how to adjust and adapt in ways that no other animal does. There is an instinctual component, but he is not circumscribed by this in the same way as other species are. G.K. Chesterton used to put this in his own distinctive way by suggesting that no explorer would pat the nose of a crocodile that had just swallowed its tenth explorer and say, 'Be a crocodile'. A crocodile cannot help being a crocodile, hence the wisdom of taking certain precautions. But man can be other than he is. We do put a hand on a friend's shoulder and say, 'Be a man', and respond when others do the same to us. We are aware of being less than our true selves, even when we are not always sure of our true selves.

It will not be possible here to go into all aspects of human life and experience that make man different from the animal kingdom, but there would be universal agreement to the statement that it has to do with consciousness.

Consciousness is a great privilege and burden. It operates in three overlapping areas. We are self-conscious, socially-conscious, and cosmically-conscious. Because of this we need to feel at home within ourselves, in our relationships and with the often forgotten or ignored cosmic dimension of being. This calls for self-acceptance, socially-conscious attitudes and behaviour, and an under-girding faith in the essential goodness of existence. For many, this latter need can find its fulfilment only in a spiritual awareness leading to specifically religious forms of expression. This was certainly what Jung discovered as being the need of his patients who were in the second half of life.

We are seldom at peace with ourselves, with different urges and goals which vary from time to time. We long to be secure in our relationships, but are not always prepared for the self-discipline and reciprocity this demands. We want to be forgiven without having to forgive. Often we feel trapped within our deepest needs, and complain that others seem indifferent if not hostile. Even when we try to invest ourselves in something beyond and bigger than ourselves, we may discover that satisfaction falls short of complete fulfilment. 'A long way from home' is the interesting title of a recent sociological (not religious) assessment of man's existential situation.

The emphasis in this chapter has been on the outer realities of life. Social forces impinge on everyone, affecting their direct, close relationships. This means that an individual's social environment needs always to be kept in view. But there are a host of inner factors: our particular biological endowment, and our idiosyncratic response to everything external to us. The important thing in our understanding of ourselves and others is to keep in mind these two sets of variables which are constantly interacting on each other. It is unrealistic to ignore either the inner or the outer world.

REFERENCES

1. Harvey Cox, *The Secular City*, Student Christian Movement Press, 1965.
2. Edgar Jackson, *Understanding Loneliness*, Student Christian Movement Press, 1980, p.66.
3. Victor Fuchs, *Who shall live?* New York, Basic Books, 1977, p.53.
4. Margaret Mead, *Male and Female*, Penguin Books, 1962.
5. Sula Wolff, *Children under stress*, Penguin Books, 1969, p.165.
6. Peter Mayhew, *Justice in Industry*, Student Christian Movement Press, 1980.
7. Alan Fox, *Beyond Contract: Work, Power and Trust Relations*. Faber, 1974.
8. Ethel Venables, *Counselling*, National Marriage Guidance publications, 1971, p.3.
9. Erich Fromm, *To have or to Be?* Abacus Books. 1978.
10. Alvin Toffler, *Future Shock*. Pan Books. 1973
11. George Gilder, *Sexual Suicide*, New York Times Books, 1973, p.1.

2 A Developing Response to Human Need

We have been looking at various aspects of the modern world, highlighting some of those factors contributing to change. Many of these aspects and factors have good elements in them and some of the changes are both necessary and right. But where these changes have created widespread distress and personal problems, there has been a variegated response over the past fifty or sixty years which has escalated and assumed a recognisable form during the sixties and seventies. In this chapter we will be examining some aspects and ingredients of that response even though it is difficult to determine where to begin and what precisely to include.

On 23rd September, 1980, an article appeared in *The Guardian* entitled: 'Sixty years of taking the dark out of the box'. It dealt with the history and work of the Tavistock Clinic, a National Health Service out-patient clinic dedicated to psycho-analytic therapy. The opening paragraph read as follows:

> The Tavistock is a clinic that uses no drugs, no sophisticated machinery, none of the expensive equipment which burdens the budgets of general hospitals. The only treatment it offers is the spoken and unspoken word because, committed as it is to the principles of psycho-analysis, it looks at unconscious mechanisms as the source of all the illness and malfunction that comes its way.

This unique clinic began in 1920, immediately following the first world war. A number of doctors were impressed by the relevance of Sigmund Freud's discoveries about the unconscious mind in relation to the treatment of shell-shock. They set about 'applying the lessons of war to the casualties of peace'. Linked initially with the famous Tavistock Square in the heart of London, it now occupies a large, modern complex in Hampstead, and logs about 25,000 out-patient attendances a year. One department is for adults, a second for adolescents, and a third for children and parents.

Dr. Alexis Brook, who is both psychiatrist and psycho-analyst, is the present chairman of the professional committee. He says, 'We're not in the business of fostering dependence. We are trying to make people — staff and clients — more independent, though, of course, in a civilised society, there's a minimal level below which you can't let people fall'.

How did Dr. Brook become interested in the kind of work for which the Tavistock is now deservedly famous worldwide? It started in Burma during the second world war. He explains:

As a newly qualified doctor, I was trained to look for illness and treat it. I had to send up figures each week of the sickness rate, malaria rate, dysentery rate, V.D. rate. To my colossal surprise and great relief nobody took any notice of me if they went up. The person on the mat was the battalion commander because towards the end of the war a few people in the Army began to recognise that these figures were indices of morals. If morale is high fewer people are ill. It was a revelation to me.

This experience created what has become a lifelong interest in the relationship between illness and the community, which reflects the direction in which the Tavistock Clinic has been moving. Hence its relevance to the theme of this book.

Counselling is a profession of the twentieth century. Some will doubt that it merits the designation 'profession' as yet, but that is the direction in which it is going. Counselling is seen by many as a watered-down psychotherapy, which view may be doing a disservice to a great deal of effective work being done with needy people. It is difficult to say where counselling ends and psychotherapy begins, and we will attempt definitions at the appropriate place and time. They are akin in that they both use precisely the same tool — the therapeutic interview.

Counselling began in the United States of America and 'most of the books on the subject have emerged from the American experience'.[1] In 1974 it was estimated there were 80,000 counsellors in America, which number must have more than doubled in the intervening years. Counselling first emerged there as vocational guidance. Richard Thoreson of the University of Missouri writes:

> Its impetus came from the American educational system; its methodology and techniques from applied psychology with emphasis on individual differences. This approach flourished during the 1930s when the emphasis was on the measurement of individual aptitudes, abilities and interests related to successful job placement. In the 1940s new concepts for practice and new objectives beyond trait-factor vocational guidance were developed. Client-centred therapy gained immediate popularity by offering a procedure through which a person by his own efforts could become a better person. This optimistic and simple approach fitted into the liberal, humanistic traditions of the United States. It is only recently that its limitations have become apparent.[2]

It was the return of the American soldiers at the end of the second world war that gave a tremendous impetus to counselling in the field of education.

Careers Advice Centres were established, usually on the campuses of Universities and Colleges. Education psychologists and university lecturers sat at tables spread all over the large lecture halls, and the G.I.s moved from one to another doing various tests and sharing their hopes and fears.

In many places it was discovered that there was no steady flow of men — there were hold-ups. Questions were asked as to why men stopped longer at particular tables, and it was discovered this was because someone was actually listening to what the returning soldiers were saying. Many of these were not so much concerned about work and education prospects. They wanted to know how they could restore their marriage relationship and get to know the two year old child whom they had never seen.

The authorities therefore established small units where men could go to talk, not about completing their education or where they might find appropriate work, but about their personal problems. These small units tended to be overwhelmed with numbers, and in 1947–48 when the authorities began cutting back on the careers units, it was discovered that students were still seeking personal help for such problems as examination neurosis etc.

Since the late fifties similar developments in the world of education have taken place in Britain. The need for student counsellors soon became apparent, and courses in counselling geared to educational settings at university and polytechnic level came into existence. Then the needs of children led to the training and employment of school counsellors. The spread of student and school counsellors is uneven, being usually dependent on the vision and financial resources of particular educational authorities.

The American churches were quick to assess the widespread need for counselling help, so teaching programmes with a religious orientation proliferated. This, in turn, influenced pastoral counselling in Britain and elsewhere.

Over the past three decades various counselling approaches have come to birth in the United States — such as Transactional Analysis, Bioenergetics, Gestalt Therapy, Psychosynthesis, and many more — and these also have been exported to the rest of the world.

An important event in counselling history as far as Britain is concerned was the commencement in 1938 of the Marriage Guidance Movement by Dr. Herbert Gray, with a group of doctors and social workers. Ten years later the official Denning Committee described the Movement as 'the most striking civilian development of recent times'. The National Marriage Guidance Council has two fields of endeavour — counselling, in connection with remedial work, and education for family life. This latter takes the form of preparing engaged couples for marriage and leading discussions in youth clubs and schools.

Helping those with marital problems is the most widely known aspect of the Council. Counselling, or remedial work, is undertaken by part-time 'marriage counsellors', whose selection and training is more rigorous than that of any other voluntary social workers. These counsellors are usually married men and women, mainly in early middle life, who have been sponsored by one of the local marriage guidance councils, passed a selection board arranged by the National Council, and taken its training.

Those desiring help must seek it personally. Counsellors do not visit people in their homes. Sometimes a wife will come with the request that the counsellor will give her husband a good talking to, or a husband will want his wife told to stop nagging. Counsellors do not impose a solution or apportion blame. It is not a case of laying down the law or sitting in judgment.

The counsellor helps, first of all, by listening. For a distressed person to be able to pour out pent-up feelings can be of great therapeutic value. He then seeks to help the couple understand their own feelings about the situation and, as a result of new insight and understanding, move forward to make their own decisions. The counsellor may refer clients to a medical, legal or spiritual consultant.

Much unhappiness can be avoided if, before the wedding day, partners are able to communicate with each other about all aspects of married life. To meet this need, marriage preparation courses are arranged in Marriage Guidance Centres, local vicarages, or the homes of counsellors. They consist of three or four meetings of two to ten couples who discuss, under the leadership of a counsellor, such aspects of marriage which are well-known causes of friction. These include religious beliefs, ignorance and insensitivity about sex, family planning, money, the question of the wife going out to work, and relationships with the in-laws. These couples are likely to bring into their relationship attitudes towards others, ideas about sex, and views about money which they acquired in early adolescence. Education for family life needs, therefore, to start in the classroom.

In recent years an increasing number of requests have come to the Marriage Guidance Council from schools and youth clubs for the services of Marriage Education Counsellors to lead discussions on the subject of personal relationships. These are not merely sex talks, but aim at helping young people in all matters of relationships with others. The emphasis is on moral *education* rather than *instruction*, helping them to make their own moral choices rather than imposing standards of conduct upon them.

Another exciting development in the field of counselling was the founding of the Samaritan movement by the Reverend Chad Varrah, Rector of St. Stephen's, Walbrook, in the city of London, in 1953. Its main purpose was to bring help, friendship and support to those people who were in such despair as to be contemplating suicide. It now has a more general function.

How do Samaritans work? Their priority is for someone to be at the end of a telephone all the time, to be a sympathetic listener prepared to go on listening as long as the caller pours out his feelings. In this way tension is broken and he may begin to see that he has more than one option open to him. The Samaritans do their best to make the caller feel that here, at last, is the certainty of caring friendship and new hope.

Sometimes an interview is arranged at the centre, or at a venue convenient to the caller. In an emergency one of the 'flying squad' will bring him, or her, to the centre, where he will be seen by one of the more experienced members, and encouraged to talk more freely about his troubles. Further counselling is arranged if this is felt necessary, but the most important thing at this stage is the selection of a 'befriender'. This is carefully made to suit the client. Befriending is the basis of Samaritan work, and the 'befriender' remains in close contact until help is no longer needed or wanted.

Samaritans are all volunteers and belong to no one religious denomination. They work as a team — Anglicans, Catholics, Salvationists, Baptists, Jews, Methodists, etc., and some who profess no particular religious faith. They are one in believing this is a job crying out to be done. No specific qualification is required except concern for their fellow-men and women, and the ability to convey it. They do go through an initial training course.

It has already been noted that Freud, unknowingly, played his part in the creation of the Tavistock Clinic. All modern forms of dynamic psychotherapy, psycho-analysis, family and marital therapy, or the modified individual and group psychotherapy, owe a debt to Freud and others who in the early years of the twentieth century were preparing the ground for what was to come. But even prior to Freud the ideas of emotional catharsis and talking therapy were around. To our certain knowledge they go back to Aristotle at least!

In Christian history there has been the Catholic confessional, and all great drama and literature is founded on the conflict between our feelings, wishes and memories. But it has been the work of Freud and some of his early and later disciples who, during the present century, have widened our understanding of human nature — increasing rather than decreasing its complexity in the process — and providing us with tools with which to offer help towards self-understanding and self-direction.

In the inaugural address to the Standing Conference for the Advancement of Counselling, October 1971, Dr. J.D. Sutherland (Consultant Psychiatrist at the Royal Edinburgh Hospital, and sometime Director of the Tavistock Clinic) said:

> Like most social phenomena the sources of the counselling movement are many, and they are clearly inter-related. I believe the major initiating stimulus was the result of Freud's discoveries. Freud made sense of what in people was dark, mysterious, irrational and, above all, frightening. He showed how the psychological disorders in the person could be correlated with failures in his social development. In the light of his views, the traditional moralistic attitude towards much human behaviour, suffering and weakness could not be maintained. Strange thoughts, feelings and actions could be understood, and if these did not vanish after their nature and origins were elucidated, they could often be managed better.[3]

At an earlier conference in January 1971 that led to the establishment of the Standing Conference for the Advancement of Counselling, Sir George Haynes had said that 'counselling was not an ephemeral concern, but a deep and pressing need of contemporary society'.

In 1978 the Standing Conference became the British Association for Counselling, the object of which is to bring together counsellors operating in different fields. It is seen as an 'umbrella' movement. In early 1980 it had 2400 individual members and over 190 organisational members. It has seven divisions:

Pastoral Counselling,
Family/Personal/Marital/Sexual Counselling,
Youth Counselling,
Counselling at Work,
Counselling in Educational Settings,
Counselling in Medical Settings,
Student Counselling.

Its objectives are —
(a) to promote and provide education and training for counsellors working in either professional or voluntary settings, whether full or part-time, with a view to raising the standards of counselling for the benefit of the community, and in particular of those who are the recipients of counselling.
(b) to advance the education of the public towards awareness of the part counselling can play generally, and in particular to meet the needs of those members of society whose development and participation in society is impaired by mental, physical or social handicap or disability.

Counselling has been variously described and defined, but the following is the definition produced by its 'Standards and Ethics Committee', and agreed to by the British Association for Counselling:

People are engaged in counselling when a person, occupying regularly or temporarily the role of 'counsellor' offers or agrees explicitly to give time, attention, and respect, to another person or persons temporarily in the role of 'client'. The task of counselling is to give the 'client' an opportunity to explore, define and discover ways of living more satisfyingly and resourcefully within the social grouping with which he identifies.

Alongside those developments that resulted in the birth of the British Association for Counselling, ran parallel developments in the varied areas covered by the different divisions of the wider organisation.

The authors of this book have been particularly involved in the pastoral counselling field during the nineteen seventies. Most of the major churches have also been involved in this work. In 1970 the Reverend Dr. William Kyle (Methodist) brought into existence the Westminster Pastoral Foundation which not only offered counselling help to all seeking it, but in addition, soon became an important training base.

During that same year members of other main denominations who were interested and, in varying degrees, already involved in counselling work, came together to form an Association which later became known as the Association for Pastoral Care and Counselling. Professor (now Sir) Desmond Pond, Head of the Psychiatric Department at London Hospital became its first President, and Canon Derek Blows, then responsible for in-service training of the clergy in the Southwark Diocese, and now Director of Westminster Pastoral Foundation, its first Chairman.

In the early seventies Father Louis Marteau established the Dympna Centre, initially for the counselling of Roman Catholic priests, but soon included ministers of other denominations and members of religious orders of the Judaeo-Christian faiths. At the same time, we were commencing a Counselling Service within the Salvation Army and a training course in Pastoral Counselling for Salvation Army officers.

There can be no doubt that over the past ten years those who have been working together to help create and then develop the Association for Pastoral Care and Counselling have built up relationships of trust, confidence and considerable depth. The shared quest has brought its own enrichment. Realisation that one is not alone in a particular task proves to be a rock of support and strength. Banishment of a sense of isolation is an incomparable boon.

In a company of people who are committed to a counselling approach to the human condition, the denominational differences do not constitute a barrier. There has been a close association between Anglicans, Roman Catholics, Jews, Salvationists, Methodists, Baptists, members of the United Reformed Church, and the Church of Scotland. It is sometimes said that counsellors feel closer to their fellow-counsellors from other denominations than they do to some of their fellow-members.

Here is a genuine ecumenism. The oft-repeated statement that there is more uniting Christians of various denominations than dividing them, is here, in the counselling world, a living experience. Counsellors and clients meet simply as fellow human beings, sharing the same existence. One of the benefits of this kind of interaction at depth is that when counsellors meet they, too, become aware of the common humanity they share, and in consequence even important theological and denominational differences are seen in perspective, or seem to disappear altogether.

The Association for Pastoral Care and Counselling became the first division within the British Association for Counselling.

REFERENCES

1. P.M. Hughes, *Guidance and Counselling in Schools*, Pergamon Press, 1971.
2. Richard Thoreson, *British Journal of Guidance and Counselling*, July 1974, p.173.
3. J.D. Sutherland, *Some reflections on the development of counselling services*, National Council of Social Service (now the National Council for Voluntary Organisations), 1971, p.4.

3 What Does Counselling Offer?

One definition of counselling has already been offered, and others will follow. The problem with the word 'counselling' is that everyone imagines that he understands its meaning, when it often becomes clear that no two people use it in exactly the same way. The word has long been part of our language, but the rapid and diverse growth of counselling activity already outlined seems to have created confusion rather than clarity.

Ethel Venables begins her book entitled simply, *Counselling* thus:

> The word 'counsel' has returned to these shores, a little debased, perhaps, by its commercial connections. Florists and the makers of spectacle frames now offer to 'counsel' us on the appropriate use of their products, but here we are discussing its use in relation to more serious dilemmas . . . It springs from the same root as consul, consult, conciliate: it suggests deliberation, a two-way process, an inter-change.[1]

The individual can hardly be too careful to whom he turns for counselling. Chaucer's advice, 'Take no counsel of a fool' makes sense. But can the folly or wisdom of someone designating himself 'counsellor' be assessed? Much thought is being given to the safeguarding of the client, for well-meaning incompetents, misguided enthusiasts, and actual charlatans undoubtedly exist.

'Man is the only animal that can be *bored*, that can be *discontented*, that can feel evicted from paradise', wrote Erich Fromm[2], and continued, 'Man is the only animal for whom his own existence is a problem which he has to solve and from which he cannot escape'. Because of this our predecessors used to turn automatically to the church. Where else was there to go? Today's secularised world has provided us with alternatives, for better or for worse. The church is still there, of course. In spite of everything that has happened to take and keep people away from it, its ministers are as busy or busier than ever. But when something has gone wrong, the first port of call for many today is likely to be the general practitioner, the social worker, the psychiatrist or the counsellor. They have become today's priests, which is a heavy responsibility for anyone or any group to carry. No wonder that many break down under the strain, so that one of today's urgent questions is, 'Who helps the helpers?'

In his seminal book, *The Faith of the Counsellors*[3], Paul Halmos demonstrates that the fall in church attendance has been paralleled by a rise in the size of the caring professions. A consequence is the search by existing helping professions for greater understanding and skill, because of the belief that a caring relationship can be used for the purpose of exploring the nature of their clients' difficulties.

This has also affected the church, in that many of its ministers (out of either desperation or genuine concern, or a mixture of both) have embarked upon counselling training courses in the hope of making their ministry more relevant and effective. This can create vocational problems in that they may feel they are no longer preaching the gospel, but simply helping people towards a greater emotional stability. There is much heart-searching among minister-counsellors. Is the one-time 'cure of souls' being lost in the process of listening to those with marriage difficulties, sharing the grief of the newly bereaved, and helping the anxious and depressed to a new self-understanding? The non-believer may shrug his shoulders and say, 'Who cares?', but these are serious questions to be wrestled with by many sensitive people.

The essence of counselling is the attempt to make the act of helping more effective by basing it on such knowledge of the human personality — its making, unmaking and remaking — as can be contributed by the various schools of contemporary psychology. This knowledge may not be *all*-important, but important it is. The effective counsellor needs also to be equipped by temperament and training, but psychological theory is not to be despised.

There is comfort in the realisation that everyone has personality problems. We are all continuously in the process of re-adjusting the tensions within us. In a sense, no one is completely 'normal' all the time. For example, who has not at some time or another crossed the road to avoid meeting a particular person. We've probably had the grace later to feel ashamed of ourselves for wanting to avoid someone we know. At that moment we had fallen short of what could be called 'normal' behaviour. But suppose we found ourselves dodging more and more of our acquaintances, and beginning to stay at home in order not to meet anyone at all, then we would probably challenge ourselves, recognising something decidedly neurotic in our behaviour.

You will notice that we put the word 'normal' in quotation marks. Its use usually creates problems. After all, what *is* normal? Our 'normal' may be quite legitimately different from your 'normal'. Rollo May says:

> The norm is a standard drawn from our knowledge of the possibilities in a situation; it is partly based upon the range of expectation, but like physical health it is not a limiting category. It is possible to measure what is wrong or unhealthy in personality, for the neurosis leads the sick person into all kinds of errors, but we cannot measure 'rightness' in this area. We can only free the individual to develop according to his own unique form. Thus being normal does not at all mean becoming static or 'average' or fitted into the same pigeon-hole with everyone else; it means just the opposite of this. The norm for personality is in a sense the ideal; and it is based upon principles of creativity and individuality . . .[4]

So 'normal' is very different from 'average'. The average man or woman does not exist, because uniformity is non-existent. Procrustes is supposed to have stretched or chopped down his guests to fit the bed he had constructed. Next morning he measured them up before they left and wrote a learned paper 'on the uniformity of stature of travellers' for the Anthropological Society of Attica!

Counselling does not generalise, but particularises. It discriminates. It concentrates on the individual. In this respect, it is of the nature of love at its highest. Love takes from the mass; it isolates and then focusses on the one. This is why in spite of today's moral climate, monogamy still has a tremendous appeal as the ideal for marriage. It is the love of one man for one woman; one woman for one man.

Counsellors should not need to remind themselves of the individuality of their clients, because each of them demonstrates the fact in every session. The counsellor is not a storehouse of general remedies for general complaints. This can be one of his temptations, of course. He may imagine he can quickly diagnose the trouble, and so jump to conclusions on insufficient and half-digested information. On any reckoning this is wrong, and can prove disastrous.

Problems may appear similar and yet have different origins, and even if the origins are the same, the different situations of particular clients will necessitate an individual approach. Clients should never become 'cases'. The word 'case' can depersonalise a relationship, and thinking of others as 'cases' can be a way of keeping them at a distance, emotionally. We make real contact only with individuals. Speaking of 'cases' may be just jargon, but it can also become an escape mechanism.

To appreciate the individuality of people involves sensitivity. This comes naturally to some, but sensitivity can be cultivated. Many people believe themselves to be more sensitive than they actually are. Feeling we are sensitive is no sure guide.

Being aware of others means noticing their reactions and being concerned about them. It means thinking of them in an imaginative way. It means remembering that how we think they should feel and react may be no true indication as to what in fact is going on inside them. Yet 'to sit where they sit', to feel as they feel, to see as from their viewpoint, is the counsellor's essential task.

Counsellors need to check on themselves from time to time, particularly in their relations with other people. If they find, for instance, that they regularly upset others, always having to explain that they have been misunderstood and did not mean to imply this or that, it is possible they are lacking in sensitivity. On the other hand, the fact that this kind of thing is not happening is no cause for complacency, because it is possible to be so insensitive as to be making no living contact at all with anyone.

Counsellors, too, are individuals. Each has his or her own way of communicating. Each has his or her own fears, anxieties and relationship problems. A counselling relationship means an involvement at depth between two unique personalities, and no one can listen to another person's unburdening without responding emotionally. Because hidden depths may be stirred in the counsellor, his self-knowledge needs to keep pace with his experience. We all like to imagine that we know ourselves perfectly, but here we are self-deceived. We certainly have inside information of ourselves, but we also have inside *mis*-information. At times we may use our reason to falsify the facts rather than to allow them to lead to fuller self-understanding.

If a counsellor is not learning about himself, he should give up counselling. It is now generally recognised that all counsellors need ongoing supervision, which will inevitably contain within it a therapeutic dimension, so that they come to terms with their enlarged self-awareness. For example, a counsellor desiring to refer a particular client to someone else is wise to probe his own feelings. What spring of emotion has been touched within him? And why? It has been said that self-exploration is like 'un-building the pyramids' — the removal of one brick or slab reveals a still larger surface beneath.

Some of the points raised in this chapter so far will be taken up and explored in greater detail later. Here we wish to concentrate on the specific question: What exactly does counselling offer to those seeking help?

Those coming for counselling are in trouble of some kind, and trouble isolates people. People in trouble tend to concentrate on what is perplexing them. If serious, the trouble will crowd out all other considerations. If not serious, it may be hovering in the background of consciousness, but still affecting the whole of life. There will be moments when it needs to be faced.

Whether the concern is with physical illness, emotional distress, economic pressures, anxiety over those close to them, or any other of life's manifold perplexities, there can be a lowering of the tone of their customary life and this can have the effect of making them feel cut off. Their pains, worries and fears close them in upon themselves, and circumscribe their individual worlds. The internal and external pressures give a sense of aloneness, and relationships suffer in consequence.

At such times it is not always possible — it may not even be desirable — to spill over to those nearest to them. Perhaps deep down they sense their own need for an objectivity they may have lost, and it is precisely this that counselling can and should provide.

Counselling is a response to a need, and the need is usually some kind of breakdown. To trace the cause or origin of the breakdown may lead to the recognition of a failure within the family, or the client's social situation. Somewhere, something has been missing, or was missed, along the line of family, society or friend relationships. Ways of coping may not have been learned or, if learned, have broken down. The client is in need of ordinary care, and counselling is such a provision. It is more than this, but this it must be. Counselling is concerned with the stuff of daily life and the particular problems arising from and within the day to day business of living.

'Alienation' is one of today's 'in' words. It is an ugly word describing an ugly, frightening reality. Rollo May describes one of his clients:

> She arrived for her therapy hour one day having just come from an art exhibition, to tell me she had discovered the symbol most accurately describing her feelings about herself: the lonely figure of Edward Hopper, in his paintings in which there is only one figure — a solitary girl usherette in a brightly lighted and plush but entirely empty theatre; a woman sitting alone by an upper window in a Victorian house at the shore in the deserted off-season; a lone person in a rocking-chair on a porch not unlike the house in the small city in which my patient grew up. Hopper's paintings, indeed, give a poignant meaning to the quiet despair, the emptiness of human feeling and longing which is referred to by that cliché 'alienation'.[5]

There are many and different causes of alienation, but Erik Erikson (whose concept of the eight stages of life constitutes the basis of chapter 9) makes the point that at each stage of life the drives of the inner being can move in positive or negative directions. If, throughout the passing of the years, the negative accumulates and outruns the positive, life will end in alienation and despair.

This has always happened to vulnerable people. It is still happening. There seems little point in trying to establish whether or not it is happening more than it did in the past. What is incontrovertible is that it is happening a great deal, and everyone suffering from alienation, loneliness and despair stands in need of help. W.H. Auden once remarked, 'Ascribe it to prevenient grace, intuition or sheer luck, one of the greatest things in any life has been the meeting of the right helper at the right time'. It follows from this that one of life's greatest tragedies is *not* having met 'the right helper' at the right time. It cannot be doubted that for many 'the right helper' has been a counsellor.

Now if the basic trouble is some form of alienation, which may express itself in many ways and lead into diverse problem areas, what the client needs is a new, positive sense of belonging somewhere and to someone. Counselling responds to that need by offering a place to share at depth, and this involves the counsellor in being totally available to the client, and in listening in a way uncharacteristic of this day and age.

Listening is the most important thing the counsellor does, which is something the beginner in this field usually finds difficult to grasp. He imagines that people come for specific advice. Many do, but the giving of specific advice is not counselling. The beginner imagines that his clients will go away disappointed if he does not quickly produce some penetrating insight, some life-transforming word of wisdom. And some will. Nevertheless, the beginner will soon learn that in the long run he does more good by listening than by anything else he does.

Listening is an art, a discipline, a science. People come to the counsellor to be heard. If a counsellor is a good listener very few of his clients will go away without feeling helped. Most counsellors are at some time thanked for giving advice that has never passed their lips. Listening is itself a form of communication. Being listened to is for most an unusual experience and often proves to be the only therapy they need.

A common complaint today is that there is no one to listen. General practitioners may not have sufficient time. Social workers find themselves with too great a work-load. Psychiatrists are still thin on the ground and very expensive. Those in the National Health Service are so overloaded that the most some of them can give to a patient is ten to fifteen minutes every six weeks to adjust their medication. Church ministers tend to think of themselves as talkers rather than listeners.

There is the now well-known story of the psychologist who created an interesting case-history for himself and then visited one hundred minister/counsellors in turn. He took with him a stop-watch, and maintained that the longest he was ever allowed to speak was 2½ minutes!

Let us be thankful for the many exceptions there are to the above sweeping generalisations. Yet it has to be admitted that listening is not a characteristic of many personal relationships today, even though a person's well-being may depend upon being listened to — at length and in depth.

A basic fact is this: most caring people talk too much; they talk too soon; and they listen too little. A basic truth is this: a person needs help to find his own words in order to understand his own experience. The child who said, 'How do I know what I think until I hear what I say?' was being both accurate and profound. We do not *know* what we think and feel until we have struggled to define, encapsulate and articulate our thoughts and feelings. 'I know what I mean but can't put it into words', usually means, 'I don't really know what I mean'.

There are, of course, thoughts and feelings 'too deep for words', but we usually use that concept to cover the whole range of experience that needs to be brought out of the past, out of the depths, in order that we might come to terms with it by understanding it through its ventilation. It is in the holding on to something we need to let go that we damage ourselves. The idea that an open confession is good for the soul is not simply a religious one. It is a basic concept of psycho-analysis, psychotherapy and counselling. Our dark, secret, largely unknown self is the enemy of our peace of mind and holds back our psychological and emotional development. It is so often the case that the experience, the deed, the habit, the thought that the client cannot or will not bring himself to disclose holds up the healing process.

The client gets most help from what he tells himself. This is the value of repeating the significant sentence, perhaps, although not necessarily, putting it into different words. What is important is that the client needs to hear what he is saying about himself coming from someone else's lips. It is as though he only half hears it initially. The repetition compels him to listen. It is the way in which a person 'comes to himself'.

Most people are strangers to themselves. The outer has moved away from the inner, and in the long run this deceives the individual himself who comes to accept the partially unreal outer self as being the whole truth. One of the functions of counselling is to introduce a person to himself, by bringing together the outer and the inner.

Sidney Smith delighted to tell of the absent-minded Lord Dudley. 'One day he met me in the street and invited me to meet myself. "Dine with me today", he said, "and I will get Sidney Smith to meet you".' We all need to meet ourselves.

Why do we fight shy of such a personal encounter? Is it that we are afraid of the impoverished self we may find? Do we live such hectic lives in order to escape from self-encounter, as though a full diary can make up for inner emptiness?

We often try to safeguard ourselves by pretence, by wearing masks. Peter Sellers gave his autobiography the interesting title, 'The mask behind the mask'. He realised that we can continue to pretend even when seeming to reveal. Sellers fostered the idea that he was an enigma. 'Who is the *real* Peter Sellers?' he would ask, adding, 'I don't know'. One of the saddest comments made at his death came from the Boulting brothers (with whom he worked for many years). They said they were sure he *did* know the real Peter Sellers only too well, and 'it was that fact that, unhappily, tortured him to the end'. Perhaps most people at a certain level fear the truth they dimly apprehend — and so put on the bold front of pretence.

What exactly do we mean when we say of someone 'he came to himself'? What is the difference between the 'he' and the 'self'? The 'he' is what others see, what the person may even believe. It is the self-image, the personage. But there is always a part of the person that is outside the 'he', that is not identified with the 'he' — the deeper 'self', the true self, the person himself. The 'I' that stands in judgment on the 'me'.

The further the 'he' and the 'self' are apart, the greater the problem. The closer they are together the better for the person and for everyone connected with him. Counselling is involved in helping to bring the 'he' and the 'self' close together, to lessen the distance between the personage (what is shown to the world) and the person (the inner reality).

Becoming pre-occupied with others, with the outer world, may be a way of escaping the path of self-discovery. Seeing we spend more time with ourselves than with anyone else, it seems sensible and important to understand ourselves in order to get on well with ourselves. André Gide said, 'Many people suffer from the fear of finding themselves alone, so they don't find themselves at all'. We may fear an empty cavern deep down within us, or an unoccupied cavern. Either way there is no sense in pretending. Things of which we are unconscious are very much alive within us, and may be doing us much harm. What becomes conscious can be lived with and lived through. It can be kept in the 'growing area' of our experience. Deep down truth is what everyone needs, and most people need help in order to find it.

Making sense of your own life should be a high priority, if not the highest of all. For example, people laugh and cry, but this behaviour cannot be seen as 'personal' unless there is a measure of insight. We expect someone to be able to explain just why he is laughing or crying. A hyena laughs, but we do not imagine that its 'ha, ha' comes from seeing a joke. A crocodile cries after a fashion, but here again we do not attribute its tears to some insight or understanding. Personal behaviour involves reasons, therefore we should be able to make some sense of it.

Dennis Brown and Jonathan Pedden in *Introduction to Psychotherapy*[6] list four different selves:

A public self: known to others and the individual;
A blind self: known to others but unknown to the individual;
A secret self: known to the individual but unknown to others;
An unconscious self: unknown to the individual and others.

So it is clear that everyone has a great deal of work to do if self-understanding is to be one of the hallmarks of his life. Yet it should be recognised that every gain in self-awareness will eventually, if not immediately, lower the level of inner tension. Self-deception of all kinds must mean extra vigilance. The so-called lie-detector is built on the principle that we are oriented towards the truth, so that every deception raises the level of anxiety. Violate the truth and measurable bodily changes occur, such as increased blood pressure, more rapid heart beat, faster and shallower breathing, lowered skin temperature (cold sweat), less salivation, and muscular tension. Deception, including self-deception, leads to some kind of inner bondage. It was Jesus who said, 'The truth shall make you free'.

All barriers to self-knowledge are within. Too often we play a game of hide and seek with ourselves, but sooner or later it ceases to be a game. Counselling is an enabling process in the quest for personal truth. Many need help in order to catch themselves out in their dishonesty. A new honesty needs to be learned.

There is a prevalent fear of introspection. A letter in *The Daily Express* contained the following sentence: 'Sane, clean-living folk do not concern themselves with what may or may not go on inside their heads'. It is true that introspection can turn into self-absorption, and that is morbid. The process then becomes self-defeating. But everyone needs a 'little daily dose of self-knowledge', and it is fundamentally healthy to encourage a gentle watchfulness of ourselves.

The good counsellor, like the good gardener, does not 'dig' too soon — before the ground is ready. But if something is seen to be struggling through, he clears the surrounding area of all the rubble in order to facilitate natural growth. The counsellor does not try to wrench material from the unconscious into awareness.

The distortion of our inner world began in childhood. Adults imagine they know what children are thinking and feeling. Very often when the child tells an adult what is happening inside himself, he may well be contradicted.

Eight year old Doreen was on holiday with her family. News came that her grandfather was ill, possibly dying. Her father said they must shorten their holiday and return home. Doreen wept. Someone said, 'Fancy crying because you have to lose two days of your holiday'. Her father intervened: 'She's not crying because of *that*. She's crying because her grandfather is ill'. Doreen remained silent. She knew full well she *was* crying because of the shortened holiday, and she carried around for many years the guilt of not having corrected her father's misreading of the situation.

In a sense, Doreen was fortunate. She did not accept her father's misinterpretation of her tears. The tragedy is when the child acts on the parents' false assumptions, and starts pretending that he is other than he is, and coming to believe the pretence.

Children need to be helped to know and own their feelings. This can be done by the adults' acceptance of what the children claim to be experiencing, and by testing out their own assumptions by functioning as an emotional mirror and reflecting back feelings without any distortions. Such statements as: 'It looks as though you are very angry'; 'it sounds as though you hate him very much', enable children to recognise and admit to negative feelings of which they are frightened. By admitting to these feelings, they can then come to terms with them.

This is precisely what happens with adults in the counselling situation. An inner honesty is encouraged and experienced. What Carl Jung called 'the shadow' can be accepted, and the pretence of being better than they are, abandoned.

It is not only the shadow self that needs to be accepted. There are strengths as well as weaknesses. To go through life denigrating yourself can be as dishonest as pretending to a non-existent virtue. There is phoney black as well as phoney white. There are hidden and unknown virtues and resources in every man, and it is this that makes counselling worthwhile for both client and counsellor.

Children are not only often misinformed by their elders, they are also constantly being interrupted by them. Rarely are they allowed to share their total feelings. Interrupting is a curse that follows us through life, so that many adults rarely have the opportunity of completing their own thoughts. Interruption can block a person's mind so that he finds it impossible to finish what he has to say. They inhibit and fragment his thinking and stop up his feelings which remain as undischarged tensions.

Counsellors find that clients often use words like 'blocked', 'stuck', 'bogged down', 'hemmed in', 'knotted', to describe their feelings. Interruptions should never happen in the counselling room, because that may be the only place where the process of unblocking and unravelling can begin. So the wise counsellor will not be too anxious to talk even when the client falls silent. To make some comment or ask a question when he is brewing over his thoughts and feelings may throw him off the track. Counselling consists of the opportunity to reveal and disentangle thoughts and feelings that have been hidden away in the deep recesses of the mind, perhaps for years.

Counsellors find that there are times when it is unwise to draw on their own experiences. The client's legitimate reaction may be, 'I was talking about myself and now you are talking about yourself'. This reaction may not be verbalised but if it is felt by the client to be the case, the flow of thoughts and feelings may cease. There are ways and times when a counsellor can quite properly use his own experience but usually this is best done in an implicit rather than an explicit way. To do it explicitly may register as a denial of the uniqueness of the experience the client is sharing.

Clients need time, and counselling is the offer of a regular uninterrupted period of time for as long as this is needed by, and useful to, the client. Patient listening permits a person's experience to slow down. Gradually he comes to himself.

We have used the word 'listening' to cover the total attitude to the client by the counsellor. Gerard Egan of the Loyola University of Chicago, uses the word 'attending', arguing that 'deep interpersonal transactions demand a certain intensity of presence'. Attending seems simple but is, in fact, intensely difficult. Egan writes:

> When a person is accused of not attending, his answer is, almost predictably, 'I can repeat word for word everything you've said'. Since this reply brings little comfort to the accusor, attending must be more than the ability to repeat someone else's words. You don't want the other person's ability to remember what you've said. You want him. You want him to be present to you in a much fuller way than he is. You want more than physical (or electronic) presence. If lack of attending is disruptive of ordinary human communication, it is disastrous in helping.[7]

Attending has a whole range of physical as well as psychological aspects. When we were setting up our counselling service, a twenty-six year old schizophrenic said, 'Don't call your premises a counselling "centre". A "centre" is a word that smacks of marble slabs and officialdom'.

The physical environment in which counselling takes place is very important. It needs to be comfortable, but not too luxurious, for it is a place where important work is to be done by client and counsellor. Both should be seated at the same level with no barrier, such as a desk, between them. The counsellor's posture should be an open one which says, 'I am totally available'. The attention should not be of such an intensity as to create tension. There needs to be a relaxed element in it.

Psychological attending includes an awareness of the client's non-verbal behaviour. The face and body are always sending out messages. Two silent people may be communicating with each other. Smiles and half-smiles, grimaces, the folding of arms, the closing of eyes, the tone of voice, the wringing of hands are all cues. They sometimes say more than the actual words being spoken. This kind of total listening is demanding indeed.

It seems that whenever one statement is made about the sensitive task of counselling, it becomes necessary to balance it with a seemingly contradictory one. The contradiction is in fact only apparent.

Having emphasised the need for giving the client plenty of silent listening time, it needs to be said that a stoney silence is not to be recommended. Everything depends upon the nature of the silence, as to whether it is a dead or a living thing. A too prolonged silence can be experienced as a threat. It is not a case of 'I must be directive', or, 'I must not be directive', but 'I must be responsive and warm to just that degree that invites disclosure without interference'. Some clients get stuck if the counsellor is too silent, others if he is too reactive. If the counsellor is unsure of a client, as to whether the silence is troubling him, he can be encouraged to ask for help.

Our thoughts and feelings are often blocked and frustration follows. Social situations mean that it is not always possible or convenient fully to express all that is inside us. But if these thoughts and feelings are never expressed, the upset does not go away but remains locked up and may express itself later in all kinds of disturbing ways. We don't bury dead emotions; they remain alive in the unconscious. Unhappiness in the present may well be linked to the undischarged unhappiness that has been accumulating within us during the years that are past. Thoughts and feelings of inferiority, of disappointment, of anger — that we have long forgotten — may be affecting us today. Very often tension and fatigue are a heritage of the unworked-out past.

This is particularly true of undischarged grief. Most of us have controlled the venting of grief which should have had full and free expression. As a consequence, a new situation might call forth an emotional outburst out of all proportion to its seriousness. We may find ourselves weeping, or near to weeping, over nothing.

Eva was in her thirties. She described a childhood and adolescence of great insecurity and distress. Cruelly beaten by her father for no offence at all, she refused him the satisfaction of making her cry. She formed the habit of saying to herself, 'I'll cry tomorrow'. And tomorrow never came. Yet, in fact, tomorrow *did* come. In her thirties she was weeping the tears she should have shed long ago.

Most of us have choked back tears for years, and have created a bank of tension inside us. We all need release. Tears in counselling are invariably therapeutic, yet everyone apologises for them.

When a client is generalising about his feelings, the counsellor will ask him to be precise. If he refers to happenings that disturb him, he is asked for a concrete example. He is encouraged to go into the smallest detail; what led up to the event; what actually happened, and then what followed. By looking at the total happening, and not simply at an isolated element in it, meanings can begin to emerge, blame might well be diluted or more widely shared; the enlarged picture may help towards a feeling of release. Hurt is eased if a person lets go of the thorn to receive the whole plant.

Thoughts and feelings need to be opened out. A sustained awareness of the hurt can be a preliminary to healing. It is not simply a remembering of the wounding past that helps, but the re-experiencing of it. The counsellor has very often to say, 'Stay with the pain'. Then it is the presence of the listener that helps make the pain bearable.

The way in which the self-disclosure is encouraged and accepted, the tender reverence with which it is listened to, is what brings comfort, and eventually healing, to the wounded spirit of the client.

Effective counselling offers the client the chance of getting better acquainted with himself. This is something everyone needs but there is a surprising reluctance to seek it. It is an actual fact that the sciences developed in this order: astronomy, geology, biology, sociology, psychology. It is as though man started with the most distant reality. He still has a strange penchant for confronting last, that to which he is nearest.

One reason for this is that many people actively dislike themselves. Groucho Marx said he would not belong to a club that would have him as a member. It may have been facetiousness on his part, but any kind of self-despising is destructive. For one thing, a person who despises himself has no real court of appeal. If others commend him, he discounts this, clinging perversely to his negative self-assessment. His hopelessness needs to lessen before he can be helped, before his self-contempt can diminish. He needs to take a more lenient attitude towards himself.

It is axiomatic that the significance of our existence is to be fully and completely ourselves. But if we truly cannot bear ourselves, we are in a dilemma. Is the dilemma hopeless? The fear that it might be, needs to be kept in check. If there is perilous stuff buried deep within us, is it not better to be aware of it? It must be necessary and important to understand as fully as possible the sources of our own life. We need more concern about the self within, not less. The proper study of mankind is man. 'He who is a stranger to himself, lives in a world of strangers'.

Because he is valued within the counselling relationship, the client can begin a new self-valuing and this in turn will lead to the inner strength to discover even unwelcome truth about himself. He will no longer have such need to project his hostility outwards on to others, but self-understanding will enable him to be self-critical in a positive way.

At the first meeting of his class, a brilliant and unpredictable university lecturer used to write on the blackboard: 'Which of the required reading for this course do you find least interesting?' The ten minutes allowed for this congenial task was insufficient. Criticism is so much more blessed to give than to receive. But then the lecturer put a second question on the board: 'To what defect in yourself do you attribute this lack of interest?' A much more difficult subject.

Making sense of ourselves, of our behaviour, of our judgments, are hallmarks of maturity. Counselling is concerned with life's maturing processes. One of these is the attaining of an increasingly objective attitude towards ourselves, learning to laugh at ourselves, to see ourselves from the outside, as it were. This is our only hope of developing a self from which there is no need to get away. The only people who are never lonely are those who are genuinely on speaking terms with themselves. It is then possible to be thankful for your own existence.

The title of this chapter is: What does counselling offer? It offers an opportunity for self-exploration and self-understanding.

The emphasis in the chapter has been on the listening of the counsellor. Listening leads to understanding, which brings compassion, which develops into love, which can issue in inner healing.

REFERENCES

1. Ethel Venables, *Counselling*, National Marriage Guidance Council, 1973, p.1.
2. Erich Fromm, *Psychoanalysis and Religion*, Bantam Books, 1967, p.31.
3. Paul Halmos, *The Faith of the Counsellor*, Constable, 1966.
4. Rollo May, *The Art of Counselling*, Nashville, Abingdon Press, 1967, p.40.
5. Rollo May, *Love and Will*, Fontana, 1974, p.68.
6. Dennis Brown and Jonathan Pedder, *Introduction to Psychotherapy*, Tavistock, 1979, p.54.
7. Gerard Egan, *The Skilled Helper*, Wadsworth Publishing Co., 1975, p.61ff.

4 The Heart of the Matter

Counselling takes many forms and operates in such diverse situations, that confusion and uncertainty regarding it is not surprising. Louis Marteau tabulates four kinds of relationships:

(a) *Pedagogic Relationships*
   The focus of the teacher is on information and clarification and is directed towards the intellect of the students. However, even in this setting, the relationship of the teacher to the students may be of some importance in the field of general or individual education.

(b) *The Counselling Relationship*
   The focus of counselling is on those areas of conscious conflict which arise from external or internal stress which is of an individual and personal nature, i.e. a specific stress for this individual. The help is focussed on the problems of which the individual is perfectly aware, although the counsellor must bear in mind the deeper, unaware forces.

(c) *The Psychotherapeutic Relationship*
   The focus of psychotherapy is on a specific area of unconscious conflict, bearing in mind that this is only a facet of the total personality. In this process the therapist makes positive use of the transference, or of a working alliance, through which the individual is helped to an emotional awareness of the underlying conflict. Here the relationship will imply the ability to make positive use of the transference situation . . . (For an explanation of 'transference' see chapter 6.)

(d) *The Analytical Relationship*
   Classical analysis focusses on the 'neurotic transference' itself and is directed towards the unconscious make-up of the individual and towards the total reformation of unconscious framework. Here the need is for an ability to sustain and control such a relationship at a very deep level.[1]

At this point it might be useful to differentiate between the terms psychiatrist, psychoanalyst, psychologist, and psychotherapist.

The psychiatrist is a qualifed doctor who has moved on to post-graduate training in the treatment of emotional and mental disturbances. He will have had some training in psychotherapy but tends to call on the assistance of clinical psychologist, social worker, or occupational therapist. Increasingly psychiatrists, psychotherapists and counsellors are working together. Counsellors very often find that their clients see a psychiatrist every month or six weeks for about ten to fifteen minutes so that the effectiveness or otherwise of their medication can be assessed and changes made if necessary.

The psychoanalyst may or may not be medically qualifed. If he is he will usually have trained as a psychiatrist before going into personal analysis and eventually being recognised by an institute of psychoanalysts. Other analysts come from psychology and social work backgrounds and it seems that this group is likely to increase in the future.

The psychologist has a degree in psychology and is not usually medically qualified. After graduation he may specialise in academic, educational, industrial or clinical psychology. Many of the latter gain their experience in psychiatric hospitals by joining the psychiatrist's team of helpers.

The psychotherapist is in a less clearly defined group. The designation implies no generally accepted training as yet, but this is likely soon to change. The Foster Report (1971) recommended that a register should be set up of those trained by certain established institutes and eventually this will be the case. J.D. Sutherland defined psychotherapy in this way: 'By psychotherapy I refer to a personal relationship with a professional person in which those in distress can share and explore the underlying nature of their troubles, and possibly change some of the determinants of these through experiencing unrecognised forces in themselves'.[2]

Everyone in the helping professions needs to develop a psychotherapeutic attitude and familiarise himself with the simpler psychotherapeutic method. It is clear that counselling and psychotherapy have a considerable overlap and, in spite of the quotation from Louis Marteau above, there are no clear dividing lines. The Marriage Guidance Council encourage their counsellors to stay in the area of conscious material, but in most long term relationships this is not possible — unconscious material is bound to break through. Then, presumably, simple counselling moves into the more complex psychotherapy realm. There can be no sharp dividing line between these two activities. Counselling and the more complicated psychological help merge into each other. At the beginning of a counselling relationship it is not always possible to say in advance what any client may need.

Before proceeding to what the title of this chapter has called 'the heart of the matter', perhaps a word should be said about 'behaviourist counselling' or 'behavioural therapy'. This involves an application of learning theory and stems originally from the Russian scientist, Pavlov, whose work on conditioning and reconditioning is reasonably well-known. The behaviourist studies the person from the outside. What the human organism does is what matters supremely. He asks 'How is it organised to do the things it does? If this needs changing, how can its present behaviour be modified or changed?'

Man is here regarded as a complicated machine, the working of which, having been studied and understood, can be adjusted if needs be. Behaviourism is an attempt to turn psychology into an exact science.

The behaviourist describes all behaviour in terms of stimulus and response. Man does not act, he reacts. He is operated by reflexes to which he has been conditioned so, if for some reason a different reaction is desirable, the process of reconditioning the reflexes should be put into operation. Behaviourism even regards depression as 'learned helplessness', and believes that new learning processes are what is needed.

Behaviourism is deterministic. As man is made, genetically and environmentally, so he must act. It maintains that man has few unalterable patterns, so the general nature of his behaviour can be changed by an elaborate process of starving the old stimuli and feeding him new and more appropriate ones.

It would be idle and unintelligent to deny the degree of truth contained in these ideas. From our, the authors', point of view, the mistake of the behaviourists is in imagining that the whole of the human personality can be explained and accounted for in this way. Man is not an automaton set in motion by certain stimuli and totally conditioned to particular behaviour patterns. There is a field of objective moral, intellectual and spiritual values that can influence man's judgment, helping him to adjust his behaviour to take account of those values. The crucial question behaviourists need to answer is: On what grounds do they claim that one pattern of behaviour is better than another? Where does the recognition of the need for change, and where does the desire for that change to take place enter the behaviourist world of stimulus/response and conditioning?

The behaviourist attacks symptoms and ignores inner causes. If he succeeds in knocking out a symptom (and he's very successful in certain areas of human behaviour) and another symptom appears, he turns his attention to the second symptom, and so on. He approaches the personality through the body, depending on physical treatments, such as drugs and electro-convulsive therapy and mechanical re-learning processes.

In contrast to this approach, dynamic psychology (Freudian, Jungian, Adlerian, etc.) is concerned with discovering causes and making inner adjustments. Attempts are made at reconciling the two positions.

For the purpose of this book, however, the authors will set aside the behaviourist position, because we feel it tends to diminish and belittle man. It concentrates on the changing of external behaviour patterns, seeing these as the whole of personal reality, ignoring the subjective world that constitutes our essential humanity. (There is a further consideration of the deterministic viewpoint of the behaviourists in chapter 5.)

Counselling is concerned with problems in which a reasonably well-integrated person requires special help. The problem may arise from his personal relationships, or be concerned with matters relating to his education, vocation or work situation. Problems may arise from within the personality, or from external circumstances. Physical factors may be involved, or the marriage relationship threatened by some deterioration from within, or the possible or actual intrusion of a third party from without. A new experience of separation, of bereavement, of loneliness, an accident or the onset of disease, a sense of sheer monotony and emptiness of life — any of these can create a personal crisis that an individual feels it impossible to handle on his own.

So, usually, it is a problem (or several problems) that brings a person into counselling. But what happens then? The counselling centres on the person, rather than the problem. The counsellor does not set out to advise, sort out, find answers, encourage a particular course of action, or do something for or to the client. His task is otherwise. It is to stimulate the resources of the other's personality, and perhaps to help him, where necessary, to alter attitudes and behaviour patterns. The client needs to move towards a more mature way of life, so the answer must be his, not the counsellor's. The solution must come from within the client. Magic solutions are not on offer.

Here we are approaching the heart of the matter. Perhaps the simplest definition of counselling is that it is the offer of a therapeutic relationship.

Writing of psychotherapy — and we have already seen that it is not possible to put counselling and psychotherapy into different categories — the late Harry Guntrip[3] wrote: 'Psychotherapy is a personal security-giving relationship which offers the patient a chance to outgrow fear, and in which therefore a method of investigation can be used to bring the relationship to bear at the important points where the patient experiences conflict, tension and anxiety'.

What, then, is this method of investigation? It is the psychotherapeutic interview. The client is free to tell his own story in his own way. Patience is one of the hallmarks of the good counsellor. He will not try to hurry the story along. He knows that it may take time for the client to reach and then open up the really painful areas. The most important sharing may not come easily or quickly. The counsellor is prepared to wait.

Some people are initially unable to articulate their feelings; others habitually understate their problems. Few are used to reflecting on their inner world or expressing and defining their feelings. The wells of affliction are often deep. Thought may be slowed up, and it may be that progress belongs to the future, not the present.

By the attentiveness of the counsellor, the client is encouraged to proceed. At certain points the counsellor will reflect back to the client what he sees is significant. He may have to ask for clarification at this point or that. He may also have to tease out what the client means by some of the words he uses, because he dare not assume that they both mean precisely the same when speaking of, say, anxiety or depression.

Careful listening and patient waiting usually brings positive results in the long run. The client has, perhaps, for some time been inexplicable to himself, an accumulation of problems, a mass of contradictions. In the counsellor he has discovered someone who can imaginatively enter into his complex world, share his feelings of disturbance and chaos, and not be overwhelmed. A new understanding dawns, and with it fresh hope. This new secure relationship holds within it an undreamed of possibility. A sense of inner freedom emerges, and a potentiality for growth is tapped. It is the creative relationship that elicits the insight and opens the door to possible change. It is the key to the nature and success of the healing prospect.

This is not an equal relationship. After all, the client is seeking help. It has about it the feel of a parent-child relationship at times, and the client may very often transfer to the therapist feelings from his own past. The 'unfinished business' from his childhood becomes operative in the here and now.

This raises the question of dependence. Almost inevitably the client does, in the beginning, become dependent upon his counsellor, but this makes it possible for his personality to begin to re-grow in a natural way. Most clients become clients because there has been some failure in emotional growth. The counsellor hopes gradually to lessen the dependence. He has no intention of becoming a permanent support. His object is to make himself unnecessary.

Mary was a very nervous thirty-one year old. She had been robbed, badly beaten, and sexually assaulted whilst waiting at a country bus stop late one night.

This shattering experience had stripped her of any confidence she may have had. First of all she had to be brought to the counselling centre by a friend

— a thirty mile journey. After several visits she managed to travel to the station nearest to the centre, but dare not walk the few yards from there on her own. She had to be met and taken back to the station. Soon, however, she was able to do the whole journey alone.

Inevitably, she became very dependent on the counsellor, and phoned two or three times in a week for long conversations. These had to be limited to once a week for twenty minutes only, and eventually eliminated altogether.

After twelve months her therapy session was made fortnightly instead of weekly. Another twelve months and the time between sessions was lengthened to three weeks. Later still, a month.

Now, four and a half years on, her dependence has been completely broken. After years of idleness because of her emotional state, she is working again part-time, as a teacher. One day she said to her counsellor: 'I don't need to come any more'.

It is sometimes said that everyone entering the helping professions does so out of a need to be needed. There is no dispute about this, nor any need for those concerned to feel ashamed on that account. But counsellors should be on the alert. They may be tempted to allow a dependency to continue when it needs to be lessened and eventually terminated. It is, of course, flattering to be needed. It satisfies a longing for authority and power. Each of us has a need to feel of value, to be important to others. But it is possible to become ensnared by a genuinely needy client into a degree of dependence that may prove damaging for both. No counsellor has the right to assume the direction of other people's lives, to become their conscience, to make their decisions for them. This kind of one-sided relationship makes it impossible for the client to grow up emotionally and to develop in the important area of the will.

The counselling relationship is inevitably somewhat one-sided to start with, but the counsellor is hoping that it will become a two-sided relationship. When this happens and the client has withdrawn back into himself his dependency feeling, he can then begin to stand on his own feet and move in the direction of his own choice. The wise counsellor is happy and more than willing to see him go.

Perhaps a little more needs to be said regarding the dangerous possibility of the counsellor being trapped into caring in the wrong way. Here is one of R.D. Laing's not-so-intricate *Knots*:

There must be something the matter with him
because he would not be acting as he does
    unless there was
therefore he is acting as he is
because there is something the matter with him
He does not think there is anything the matter with him
because
one of the things that is
the matter with him
is that he does not think there is anything
the matter with him
therefore

we have to help him realise that,
the fact that he does not think there is anything
the matter with him
is one of the things that is
the matter with him[4]

Many clients are in therapy because their parents believed they always 'knew best'. As children they were never allowed to test out their own ideas, choose their own friends, make their own mistakes. It is tragic if the counsellor should take over the parents' role in this respect. The clients are struggling towards their own freedom and integrity, and the counsellor's good intention must aid that struggle, not hinder it. He must not become an auxiliary super-ego, but an auxiliary ego.

There is a corrupt counselling that can be a well-disguised form of manipulation. The possibility of this lies in the fact that the client gives the counsellor the right to influence him, but this must not become a 'take-over'. The counsellor cannot accept responsibility for the client. All he can do is accept responsibility for what transpires in the counselling room. That is responsibility enough.

Sheldon Kopp has written a fascinating book entitled *'If you Meet the Buddha on the Road, Kill Him*[5]. It should be compulsory reading for all counsellors, psychotherapists, clergy, social workers, analysts, etc. His main contention is that the guru is a menace to himself and to others. Ideally the human family consists of brothers and sisters, i.e. equals, and not parents and children. So, having said that the counselling begins in an unequal relationship, the emphasis must be made that it should end very differently, when two adults say good-bye to each other on equal terms.

Fortunate are those clients whose counsellors daily remind themselves of words penned by the 16th century Fra Giovanni (AD 1513):

There is nothing I can give you which you have not;
but there is much that while I cannot give, you can take.
No heaven can come to us unless our minds find rest
in it today. Take heaven.
No peace lies in the future which is not hidden in the
present instant. Take peace.
The gloom of the world is but a shadow; behind it, yet
within it, is joy. Take joy.

Any scaffolding the counsellor is intending to erect to support his client's wobbly structure must be strictly temporary. It is the structure itself that needs strengthening, and this must happen from within.

The counsellor is not an ombudsman, even though at times he might wish he were. His sympathies may be so aroused by what the client brings that he would love to make approaches to people and authorities outside the counselling situation in order to get circumstances changed. But this is not his function.

In *Ethical Standards in Counselling*, Joan Burnett wrote:

Counselling accepts the status quo of social and political organisation and of society's pattern of roles and relationships. This acceptance does not rest upon a value judgment. It follows from the need to establish boundaries regarding the area of concern, in order to work effectively; a selection of material, if you like. It also follows from psychoanalytic theory, which regards the primary relationships with parents and siblings as the pattern which determines the form of subsequent relationship. Counselling has to do with inner conflicts and is concerned primarily not with society and its shortcomings and ideals, but rather with the client's social perceptions and actions as reflections of his psychic health, conflicts and difficulties.[6]

Part of the counselling process may very well be to help the client to make decisions on social and political matters, but it is not the counsellor's task to take up cudgels on his client's behalf or even to specify what decisions he should make. The counsellor may, *as a citizen*, be socially and politically active, but this will be quite separate from his work as a counsellor.

The counsellor's first concern is for the individual before him. Counselling is directed towards the person's growth, independence and development. Part of that development will be the increasing ability to make decisions in the various areas of his life. Changes may take place, but they flow from the change within the client.

Most counselling is non-directive in form and content in that the client is not told what to do, what to believe in, or how to behave. But there is inevitably a directive element in that the client may be directed towards matters which, being understood in some new way, can result in a quite radical change in behaviour. The client should always be advised and encouraged to test any new insights and interpretations and subsequently reject those he does not find of value and significance.

A paper entitled 'Counselling and Political Change' was delivered by Professor Paul Halmos[7] at an international conference in 1974 and was later published under the revised title, 'The Personal and the Political'.

He argued the case strongly and cogently against those who urged that therapy today has become a commodity, a means of social control. It is true that increasingly therapists must understand the changing social and political realities and that there is a sense in which 'every human act is a social and moral statement; a political fact . . .', but this must not mean that the counselling itself becomes politically oriented. That must remain essentially personalistic.

Appreciative understanding is the essence of the counselling relationship. Rollo May writes:

> The true counsellor . . . seeks to understand people from the standpoint of appreciation. And far from objecting, people prize this kind of understanding. For it raises the prestige of the one who is understood, and helps give him a sense of worth as a person. This understanding breaks down the barriers which separate a man from his fellows; it draws the other human being for a moment out of the loneliness of his individual existence and welcomes him into community with another soul.[8]

The counsellor needs to become so absorbed in the client's story as to become to some extent identified with it. As the client tells of sad and bitter experiences at home as a child, of his inability to learn at school through being bullied and ridiculed, of his embarrassment when in the company of women, the counsellor feels with him and shares his own understanding to just the extent that is necessary for the client to feel at ease, and so able to continue.

There is nothing magical about this process, even though it may seem mysterious. After all, it happens in different ways and varying degrees almost every day. Whenever two friends share an experience, or when we watch a film, there is a tuning-in to another's world. This is the very spirit of counselling, where its operation can bring release and healing.

In *Modern Man in Search of a Soul*, Carl Jung described the merging process that results in both the counsellor and client being changed:

> The meeting of two personalities is like the contact of two chemical substances; if there is any reaction, both are transformed . . .
> Two primary factors come together in the treatment — that is, two person, neither of whom is a fixed and determinable magnitude . . . you can exert no influence if you are not susceptible to influence.[9]

This kind of participation in other people's lives yields an understanding that is far more intimate and meaningful than empirical observance or scientific study. It has about it a personal element, each person in a sense experiencing the other.

This raises the subject of influence. Books or articles in psychology magazines on 'how to influence' people need careful scrutiny. After all, influencing is a process which works chiefly in the unconscious area of a person's life. To turn it into a conscious technique may be to use it as a form of manipulation.

A better understanding of how we are ourselves influenced should enable us to protect ourselves from the effects of propaganda and/or advertising, but this is far removed from the kind of influencing that should be operating in the counselling relationship.

In a later chapter we will be studying the word 'empathy'. Here it is necessary and sufficient to point out that influence is one of the results of an empathic coming together of two people. There is an over-lapping, to some extent, of psychic states.

Influence operates in various areas. We have all known the experience of having dropped an idea into someone's mind, only to find that later they come to regard it as their own. This can be a case of stealing an idea, but very often it means we have influenced someone in the realm of ideas without their knowledge, which can either be gratifying or irritating.

Another subtle area of influencing is the way in which two people sharing together at depth, over a long period, can begin to take on each other's gestures, tone of voice and vocabulary. A certain contagion is operating, which means that within limits it is possible to put another person — or even a small group — into a particular mood by assuming that mood. The counsellor, for example, seeks to put his client at ease by initially behaving in a particular way. Whether he is successful depends on his own skill, but also on the suggestibility and susceptibility of the other.

In these and other ways we are influenced by our environment, but each selects particular items and most of this selection process happens at the unconscious level.

When thinking of the power of influence — especially as it affects a person's ideas — we should be concerned about the matter of truth. Some individuals and groups are able to believe almost anything if it happens to correspond with their own desires. Alfred Adler used to say that the public wanted to be fooled. Similarly, individuals can be enticed towards error if that is in line with their prejudices. So, even in what we have called the 'unequal' relationship that exists initially between counsellor and client, the latter will not be quickly influenced by the former unless there are already specific tendencies in his mind, probably in his unconscious. In a sense he wants to be influenced; there is a readiness to believe. Relationships get stuck if the reluctance to change is total.

At the beginning of a relationship with a new client, the counsellor does not ask himself the question: How can I treat, change, cure this person? His basic question is: How can I provide a relationship which this person may use for his personal growth and development?

It may seem too much of a generalisation, but in the last resort it is usually the elimination of fear that is required. In a later chapter Erikson's concept of 'basic trust' as the fundamental human need will be delineated and emphasised. If this 'basic trust' is not adequately established in the first year of life, ever afterwards there will be elements of fear and distrust operating with varying intensity and strength. The baby's experiencing of the mother establishes deep down within the child the degree to which in later life he will feel life is to be trusted.

In *A Rumour of Angels*, Peter Berger writes:

A child wakes up in the night, perhaps from a bad dream, and finds himself surrounded by darkness, alone, beset by nameless threats. At such a moment the contours of trusted reality are blurred or invisible, and in the terror of incipient chaos the child cries out for mother. It is hardly an exaggeration to say that, at this moment, the mother is being invoked as a high priestess of protective order. It is she (and in many cases, she alone) who has the power to banish the chaos and to restore the benign shape of the world. And, of course, any good mother will do just that. She will take the child and cradle him in the timeless gesture of the Magna Mater who became our Madonna. She will turn on a lamp, perhaps, which will encircle the scene with a warm glow of reassuring light. She will speak or sing to the child, and the content of this communication will invariably be the same — 'Don't be afraid — everything is in order, everything is alright'. If all goes well, the child will be reassured, his trust in reality recovered, and in this trust he will return to sleep.[10]

Berger goes on to ask whether or not the mother is lying to the child, and suggests that this raises basic religious questions. Some will prefer to think in 'cosmic' rather than religious terms, but what is clear is that we need in the depths of our experience a sense that not only are mother and her love dependable, but that life itself can be trusted. Uncertainty at this level produces fear.

Does any child emerge from what Frank Lake calls 'the womb of the spirit' (the first nine to twelve months of life) with an experience of total trust? No. Fear is part of everyone's inheritance from babyhood. So part of our quest in life must be the discovery of ways to handle, if not to eliminate or master, fear.

The Fearful Void is Geoffrey Moorhouse's story of his one-man trek across the Sahara desert. He undertook the journey to test himself, to explore the void that lurks within — the fear of loneliness and inadequacy, the lack of self-sufficiency and self-understanding. Moorhouse wanted to examine the extremities of his own fear. He writes of the calibre of the fear which every man carries within him, and continues:

> It appears in a great many other forms, almost every day of his life. We hesitate to speak to strangers for fear of a rebuff, a small humiliation. We are loath to act generously because we fear that more may be taken from us than we really wish to give. We will not stand up and be counted in some small but important matter because it may cost us a security or, more frequently perhaps, an advancement. Gradually we become stultified, incapable of giving to each other, waiting instead for the next hostile move from another fearful man, which must be countered with all the craft at our disposal, for the sake of self-preservation.[11]

Further in this exciting story, Geoffrey Moorhouse says something to encourage us all. In spite of his fear, he knew moments of great calm, and discovered that these followed a consistent pattern. He writes: 'This came after I had accomplished some small constructive thing'.

For many people, inhibited if not destroyed by fear, that 'small constructive thing' has been the seeking of counselling help. Fear is the enemy of inner peace. It is at the root of hate. It makes love impossible. It shuts people up within themselves. Our need is for basic trusts, for confidence at depth. The therapeutic relationship offered by counselling and psychotherapy can help an individual move in that direction. At its most complete this kind of treatment is necessarily long, because it involves a 'therapeutic regression', an experiential returning to childhood's early days in order to, in a way, begin again. The rebirth of a personality, and then its regrowth in a fundamental way, can and does occur.

The emotional needs of most people seeking counselling help are much less than this, although the principle of rebirth and regrowth belong to even short-term counselling relationships.

REFERENCES

1. Louis Marteau, *Words of Counsel*, T. Shand Publications, 1978, p.51ff.
2. J.D. Sutherland, *British Journal of Psychiatry*, 1968, 114:509.
3. Harry Guntrip, *Healing and the Sick Mind*, Allen & Unwin, 1964, p.156.
4. R.D. Laing, *Knots*, Penguin Books, 1970, p.5.
5. Sheldon Kopp, *If you Meet the Buddha on the Road, Kill Him*, Sheldon Press, 1974.
6. Joan Burnett, *Ethical Standards in Counselling*, edited by H.J. Blackham, British Association for Counselling, Bedford Square Press of the National Council for Voluntary Organisations, 1974, p.55.
7. Paul Halmos, *British Journal of Guidance & Counselling*, July 1974.
8. Rollo May, *The Art of Counselling*, Nashville, Abingdon Press, 1967, p.119.

9. C.G. Jung, *Modern Man in search of a Soul*, New York, Harcourt, Brace & Co., 1933, p.57.
10. Peter Berger, *A Rumour of Angels*, Penguin Books, 1970, p.72.
11. Geoffrey Moorhouse, *The Fearful Void*, Paladin Books, 1975, p.16ff.

5 Basic Principles

Questions and answers are meant to be linked. There is obviously no point in answering questions that are not being asked, or in evading those that are. Our argument so far is that life itself creates problems and raises questions, that these are intensified by the kind of society in which we live, and that counselling seeks to ease some of those problems, and answer some of those questions by a particular approach to individual people.

Today's world is threatened by a nuclear holocaust, but the individual may be faced with devastation of his interior life through a process of psychological, emotional and spiritual fragmentation. Modern man may hold a tight rein over the forces of nature, but if this is accompanied by the loss of himself, what hope is there? Man needs to become a unified whole if he wishes to live and act out his true humanity.

Plants and animals have an easier time of it than man. Their development and perfection does not depend upon any personal contribution. They simply express what is within and respond to what is without. Man's dignity lies precisely in the role that he himself must responsibly play towards his own fulfilment and that of his society and world. The highest expression of man's creativity is the contribution he makes toward his own self-completion.

Having looked at what counselling offers (chapter 3), what is its essence (chapter 4), here we are outlining some of its basic principles.

ACCEPTANCE

The counsellor accepts the client in such a way that could be for him a new experience. The word 'accept' has many shades of meaning. Relating to an inanimate object it means taking it into our own possession, as in the receiving of a gift. Relating to a mental concept it involves the recognition of an idea as true and/or significant. But when we use the word of a person, a whole new dimension enters into its meaning.

In the counselling world acceptance includes such attitudes as respecting, understanding and compassionately receiving. The counsellor is open-minded and open-hearted. His acceptance involves a willingness to enter into the client's world of thought, feeling and experience; it is related to the needs that have motivated the client to come to him.

Although initially there may well be concentration on limited areas of a person's life, there will be something total in the acceptance offered. The client may possess unpleasant attitudes, basic limitations, and perhaps some distressing behaviour patterns. He will be made up of negative and positive elements, but the counsellor — with full awareness of the facts — will accept the client to the utmost limit of his own capacity.

How does a person feel who is accepted in this way? He feels warm inside, safe, free to be himself, prepared to let down his guard, willing to share. He may gradually become aware of inner strengths, lose some of his fears and feel less lonely. He becomes open to what the counsellor has to offer. The possibility of regaining control of his own life and conduct seems nearer. The door to inner healing appears to be not too far away. A degree of comfort — the word really means 'with strength' — is received.

This kind of healing acceptance can be offered fully only by those for whom the human person has worth, dignity and value. It involves the recognition of man's uniqueness, and the fact that he does not forfeit his value even though he himself denies it in his own thinking and conduct. A man may not be living out his own dignity, but deep down within him that dignity exists. No bill of rights bestows this, and living in a society that does not recognise it, does not destroy it. In the counselling room two very different people of *equal worth* face each other.

This kind of acceptance can and does take place in less formal situations than the counselling room.

A timid teacher was demoralised by a rebellious fourteen-year-old who became the leader of open rebellion in the class room. One day she detained him after school and asked him why he was picking on her. For a moment he looked at her sullenly, and then said, 'Because you're such a sucker for it'.
'I know I am', the teacher replied. 'I've always been afraid of people like you ... but isn't there some other reason why you're always fighting and picking on people who can't take care of themselves? Don't you want anyone to love you or help you?' To her surprise he broke down and shared with her his own inner misery, loneliness and hostility — the sources of his rebelliousness.

What was it that created that break-through? It was the teacher's courage that enabled her to be honest about her timidity. The fourteen-year-old knew then that she was accepting him, *including his anxiety about himself and his hostility towards her.* Her ability to accept herself enabled her to accept him, and eventually made it possible for him in turn to accept himself.

Our friends are those who accept us as we are. In their company we feel at peace because there is no need to doubt our own worth; 'we are taken back into the great lap of life'.

It was in the lap of mother that our first experience of acceptance came. The baby must be accepted, held, loved, fed, sustained. When this happens he lies in his cot content, gurgling, sleeping. His acceptance by his mother is his 'being'. Later on he throws his toys over the side of the cot and pram, then moves beyond himself. But it all began with his acceptance, which led on to self-hood.

Very often because of the inadequacy of that acceptance, in later life men and women feel insecure and threatened. They need what the distressed baby needs (see the quote from Berger in chapter 4), the assurance of mother that all is well. The counsellor becomes that mother substitute.

Everyone needs to be accepted in an unqualified way, and in the client this need is often overwhelming. He may see the need for change within himself, but does not know how to proceed. Usually he is unhappy with himself, as well as his situation. He may be holding on quite desperately to a sense of his own dignity and worth, but is also aware of failure, weakness, dissatisfaction. So he comes to the counsellor fearing disapproval. He very often resents the need to seek help, and may come not intending to be fully open to the counselling process. The desire to hide part of ourselves is quite basic, especially if we are unsure how the revelation will be accepted. It is not until the client feels safe that he will be prepared for the degree of self-disclosure necessary. The counsellor must not be seen as a threat.

Just as the teacher in the above illustration accepted the young bully's hostility, the counsellor is prepared to accept the client's hostility. Much of the client's hostility may well be turned inwards towards himself, but very often some is directed towards the counsellor. Expression of these feelings in the safety of the counselling room can bring a sense of unbelievable relief. The discovery, too, that the hostility expressed does not disrupt, let alone destroy the relationship, has great value. Such acceptance is part of love.

A mother hugs her child, holding him close. He sobs out in real frustration, 'I hate you, Mummy. I hate you. You never let me stay up'. The mother holds the child still closer and says, 'I know, darling. I know'. It is out of this kind of experience that deep relationships are built. The mother absorbs the child's hostility, and healing results.

In the chapter on acceptance in *The Casebook Relationship*, Felix Biestek wrote:

Acceptance is not an all-or-nothing phenomenon, like perfect sight or total blindness. Rather every caseworker has a certain degree of skill in acceptance, and this degree may vary from day to day or from client to client. No caseworker has, or is expected to have, perfect acceptance, for that would require a godlike wisdom and immunity from human frailties. In the practice of every caseworker, however, there is always room for improvement, and there is a professional obligation to strive continually towards greater skill in acceptance of the people we serve.[1]

This paragraph precedes a list of 'impediments' to acceptance by the counsellor of the client. He lists eight of these:
1. *Insufficient knowledge of patterns of human behaviour.* The counsellor needs to know what to look for, so unless he is all the time increasing his knowledge, he may miss something of great importance.
2. *Non-acceptance of something within the self.* Unresolved conflicts within the counsellor will make it difficult if not impossible for him effectively to help the client in those specific areas.
3. *Imputing to the client one's own feelings.* By assuming a knowledge of his client's feelings because of his own, may silence the client who may experience this as a silent form of rejection.
4. *Biases and prejudices.* The tendency to label people (e.g. alcoholics, homosexuals, unmarried mothers, etc.) may lead to the counsellor not listening carefully enough to the individual client.
5. *Unwarranted reassurances.* These can prevent the client from facing reality.

To dismiss, for instance, the possibility brought by the wife of an alcoholic that something in her might be contributing to her husband's problem, may prevent her from looking at something very important in herself and in the marital relationship.

6. *Confusion between acceptance and approval.* Most clients do not approve of something in their own lives and are seeking help on that account. So, while the counsellor's acceptance should be as comprehensive as possible, this does not necessarily include approval of everything the client does. The counsellor accepts *the person*, and seeks an understanding of the reality of the situation.

7. *Loss of respect for the client.* If this happens as the client shares his story, it is unlikely that the counsellor will be able to hide the fact.

8. *Over-identification.* This may arise through a lack of self-awareness on the part of the counsellor. Seeing similarities between himself and the client, the counsellor may respond in a way which meets his own need rather than the client's.

It will be clear that this kind of acceptance which is a basic principle in counselling, is difficult to achieve and sustain. It is rare but necessary if the counsellor is to create the atmosphere that enables a client to feel secure enough to bring out into the open the disturbing aspects of his environment, and the painful facts of his own personality. The client needs to accept his acceptance by the counsellor.

CONFIDENTIALITY

Most people going for counselling will make the assumption that the information shared will be held in strictest confidence. He communicates secret information, and expects it to be kept secret. Any suggestion that all or part of it will be shared with others would inhibit him, if not close him up altogether. He needs help, but does not want to risk his reputation in order to get it.

This places a heavy responsibility on the counsellor. The preservation of confidentiality is an essential element of the relationship. Any known violation would lead to a termination of the work being done, and probably undermine anything that will already have been achieved.

The concept of confidentiality enshrines the right of every person to his own secrets. A man's inner thoughts and feelings are his alone. He is free to share them, but the recipient of such confidences has the responsibility of holding them intact. Because his inner world belongs to no one but himself, he has the right, if he chooses to make disclosures, to impose his own limitation on the use to which it can be put. Biestek writes:

> An invasion of a person's secret contrary to the owners will, even if no other damage to the owner results, is a theft. A revelation of a secret, even of one which was lawfully obtained, which is revealed in a manner contrary to the conditions imposed, is a violation of justice.[2]

Having made that categoric statement, Biestek goes on to say that a person's right to secrecy is not absolute, because 'this right, as every human right, is limited by law, by the rights of other persons, and by the rightful good of society as a whole'. To take an extreme case: If we knew in confidence that someone intended to commit murder or to explode a bomb, no one would dispute our absolute right to ensure, if we could, that these things did not happen.

The three professions where the concept of confidentiality is already operative are medicine, the law, and the priesthood. Even here the degree of trust appears to be lessening, and only lawyers have full legal protection. In *Ethical Standards of Counselling* J.S. Norell writes:

> In fact the absoluteness of the confidentiality in the doctor-patient transaction has been steadily eroded over the years. A doctor may make a proper show of resistance in, say, a divorce court, but in the end he can be directed to divulge what he knows. By contrast, in the case of two other professions who may possess 'sensitive' information the lawyer has ample protection (in law), while it is unthinkable (at present) that a priest would be exposed to this sort of pressure in public.[3]

Most people seem prepared to allow their doctors all the discretion they need. Whatever the doctors do, they feel, is bound to be in their best interests. This concept of shared responsibility and confidentiality now extends to social workers. Case conferences are generally accepted as necessary and right, and any misgiving entertained by the 'case' have to be tolerated. So this kind of shared confidentiality has come to be widely accepted as sometimes necessary and desirable.

Counselling, it seems to us, will probably need to develop along medical lines but should, in fact, have more in common with the confidentiality of the confessional. A tremendous sense of relief is experienced in the client who is assured of the complete confidentiality of what is being disclosed. Yet it has to be recognised that the counsellor may feel it necessary to seek 'outside' help. Another fact of counselling life is the recognition that counsellors do need ongoing supervision in order to function safely. J.D. Sutherland writes:

> Learning is best facilitated when one is up against a difficulty, a blockage in our understanding of what a client is bringing. What is needed then is an opportunity for the counsellor to describe his difficulty within a group he trusts. He has got to feel free to expose his confusions and secure enough to accept the implications for his own personality of the comments that others will make. This sharing of experience is best done in a group of colleagues with the assistance of a consultant, i.e. someone with more experience than the members of the group.[4]

The permission of clients should be secured before anything they have divulged is disclosed to anyone else. They need to know that even during the disclosure necessary for the sake of supervision, anonymity will be ensured. Numbers instead of names, or simply the term 'client' can be used, as happens in the Marriage Guidance Movement. The clients still have the right to claim complete confidentiality regarding particular aspects of their story which they would find intolerable to be known by anyone other than the counsellor.

In those rare instances of serious criminal behaviour the counsellor may feel it necessary to encourage the client to make whatever confession or reparation may be desirable. This may, in fact, be necessary for the client's complete healing.

ENCOURAGING SELF-DETERMINATION

One of the basic purposes of counselling is to encourage and increase the degree of self-determination in the lives and experiences of clients. Most clients — perhaps we should say 'most people' — feel themselves to be less free than they either want or ought to be. Human dignity demands personal freedom. Every man should be able to accept responsibility for living his life in such a way as to achieve both his immediate and long-term goals as he sees them.

Counselling is involved in the business of glimpsing possibilities and at the same time discovering the basic conflicts and inner tension getting in the way of their fulfilment. This means beginning with the present reality. 'I'd be alright', said a psychiatric patient, 'if it weren't for reality'. That goes for us all. But reality is what must, first of all, be faced.

Seeing the reality of your need is the first step. Simone Weil wrote: 'The danger is not lest the soul should doubt whether there is any bread, but lest, by a lie, it should persuade itself that it is not hungry'. Most people, of course, come to a counsellor because they have recognised a need. He has a hunger that is not being satsified. He may not, however, be aware of the extent of his need.

So a client needs insight, but may not be ready for it. It must have meaning for him and he must be able to use it constructively. His earlier attempts at solution should be examined, and the reasons sought as to why they were not successful, before proceeding further. He needs to gain a measure of realistic strength, and come to see his earlier hopelessness, not as springing from a factually hopeless situation, but as a problem to be understood and solved. His hopelessness needs to be modified because it leads to self-despising.

Many a person's renewal begins in learning to take a more generous attitude to himself, because hopelessness leads to 'copelessness'. Part of this learning experience must be the examination of his own share in the difficulties that are his.

It is only in this way that the client can begin to assume responsibility for himself, that allows an inner dependence to develop, leading on to a new whole-heartedness. Reality means being without pretence, being emotionally sincere, recognising that he has the capacity to change. But has he?

Any consideration of the subject of self-determination raises the question of freedom. Even if a man is self-determined, the fundamental issue remains, 'Is the self that does the determining free?' One approach to this question can be a consideration of the position of those who deny the concept of free-will.

B.F. Skinner is such a determinist. He questions and denies the whole idea of man as a free agent. He, therefore, thinks it wrong to apportion blame or responsibility for any human action. This person commits serious crimes, another serves humanity. Both classes of behaviour, argues Skinner, result from the interplay of identifiable variables that completely determine what each other does.

A man's behaviour obeys laws in the same way that a billiard ball moves when struck by another ball. He writes: 'If we are to use the methods of science in the field of human affairs, we must assume that behaviour is lawful and determined.'

This assumption clearly implies the possibility of behaviour control. Learn to manipulate the conditions and this will result in a change of behaviour. Skinner believes that the ability to manipulate behaviour can be used for the good of all.

This changing of behaviour can be achieved by *functional analysis* i.e. an analysis of behaviour in terms of cause and effect, so the causes can be controlled. According to Skinner there is no need to talk about mechanisms operating *within the organism*. The behaviour can be explained and controlled by manipulating the environment. There is no need to take the organism apart in order to look inside.

Control of behaviour is achieved by modification of the environment. There is the admission that the genetic factors can influence behaviour, but because these cannot be controlled they are to be largely ignored.

Skinner recognises that a person's behaviour pattern varies from time to time. But even if no differences in the environment can be seen to account for these variations, he refuses to countenance the idea of an internal, energising force. There is no such thing as a basic personality; only patterns of behaviour. There is no personality to change and develop; only the development of behaviour patterns.

Skinner recognises, of course, that there are abnormal behaviour patterns (although these are not blameworthy). His goal in treating such is simply to replace the abnormal with normal patterns. This can be done by the direct manipulation of behaviour. He regards such concepts as 'repressed wishes', 'identity crises', 'conflicts between ego and super-ego', as 'explanatory fiction'. He believes that undesirable behaviour can be modified by manipulating the environment — and that is all that is necessary.

What are we to make of this? Long before Skinner, Freud had been a 'hard determinist'. He believed that heredity and environment together determined everything. Freud's younger disciple, Adler, (who parted company because of difference of viewpoint) was known as a 'soft determinist'. He did not minimise the importance of heredity and environment, but believed in another factor — a 'personal' factor. He saw that different individuals made different use of the raw materials that life provided. So one deprived child will grow up trying all the time to grab, to acquire, whereas a similarly deprived child will, in later life, seek to ensure that others do not have to endure the kind of deprivation from which he suffered. The same experience can lead to opposite behaviour patterns. The determinism is 'soft' not 'hard'.

Karl Marx has also been regarded as a determinist, although he was thinking in economic rather than psychological terms. In *The Heart of Man*, Erich Fromm refutes this:

Yet neither Marx nor Freud were determinists in the sense of believing in an irreversibility of causal determination. They both believed in the possibility of change rooted in man's capacity for *becoming aware of the forces which move him* behind his back, so to speak — and thus enabling him to regain his freedom. Both were — like Spinoza, by whom Marx was influenced considerably — determinists *and* indeterminists, or neither determinists *nor* indeterminists. Both proposed that man is determined by the laws of cause and effect, but that by awareness and right action he can create and enlarge the realm of freedom.[5]

Skinner recognises that it is often desirable that man's behaviour should change. He makes value judgments. Recognising that cruelty is 'bad' and kindness is 'good', he is prepared to manipulate people into being 'good'. But he does not believe that these values have a 'moral source'. So, having experienced a better behaviour pattern, the person is not more virtuous — he just feels better, and others benefit as well. There is no need to postulate an ideal world of beauty, goodness and truth.

He gives no satisfying or convincing explanation as to how such 'moral' concepts arise at all in a completely physical world. Those belonging to Skinner's school of thought are sometimes called 'physicalists' because everything, including their thoughts, are really physical phenomena.

Skinner's preoccupation is with the outward, with external behaviour, whereas for the counsellor the important world is within. 'Only the inward journey is real'. What makes man is his inner world of feelings, desires, aspirations, hopes, fears, dreams.

There is, of course, a physical basis to man's personality, but he becomes human by transcending the purely physical. 'I know myself'. There is the self that knows and the self that is known. There is also the relationship between the two. There are two of me. 'I' can take 'myself' to task, and decide to be different.

For Skinner, whatever man *does* is what matters. For the counsellor what a man *is*, is all-important. It is true that the outward reveals the inward. But the inner reality is the reality that counts supremely.

The ideas of B.F. Skinner have filtered through into the thinking of lesser minds. Many are saying that man is essentially unfree. He is determined by the culture into which he is born and reared. Very often he becomes a pawn of ruling forces. He is daily being moulded by the media into a person of such and such opinions and belief, desired and pre-planned by others. He is simply the creature of his genes, his culture and his circumstances. Everything he does is psychologically determined.

What does this do to man? Initially it turns him into an automaton. He is no more than a particularly intricate machine. Then, later on, it makes him a puppet, because some of the 'superior' automata decide that it would be better to change him in certain ways. The self-appointed manipulators start altering this and that so that he begins to function differently. This robs him of all his value, his dignity, his basic humanity.

Professor Skinner once had an important — and now well-known — encounter with the equally famous Carl Rogers[6]. They were lecturing at the same conference, and Rogers issued his challenge. He said:

From what I understand Dr. Skinner to say, it is his understanding that though he might have thought *he chose* to come to this meeting, might have thought he had a purpose in giving this speech, such thoughts are really illusory. He actually made certain marks on paper and emitted certain sounds here, simply because his genetic make-up and his past environment had operantly conditioned his behaviour in such a way that it was rewarding to make these sounds, and that he, as a person, doesn't enter into this. In fact, if I get his thinking correctly, from his strictly scientific point of view he, as a person, doesn't exist.

In his reply, Dr. Skinner said that he would not go into the question of whether he had any choice in the matter (presumably because the whole issue is illusory) but stated, 'I do accept your characterisation of my own presence here'.

A great deal of present-day thinking suggests that man is formed and moved by forces — cultural forces without and unconscious forces within — which he does not comprehend and which are beyond his control. But is this the whole picture?

Carl Rogers says that the explanation with which Skinner concurs as to his presence at that conference, cannot be applied to human events as he, Rogers, knows them.

There is no need to dispute the view that the sequence of cause and effect operates in the psychological and emotional realms as in the physical world, but man can transcend that sequence, can himself introduce other causes and, in this way, become the creator of change within himself.

Although recognising certain limitations, man has a sense of personal freedom. One of his purposes in life should be to increase this fundamental area, to become more autonomous. Any compulsion detracts from his humanity. All compulsive behaviour is neurotic.

The motorist makes a decision regarding the pedestrian wanting to cross the road, as to whether to slow down or stop. His habit and temperament come into operation, of course, but at any given time he can break his habit of a lifetime and act, as we say, 'out of character'.

We tend to think of freedom in relation to outward alternatives, but essentially it is an inner thing. In his book, *From Death Camp to Existentislism*, Viktor Frankl vividly describes his experience in the concentration camp where everything — possessions, identity, choice — was taken from him. Months and years in that environment showed that there was one thing — the last of the human freedoms — that could not be taken away: *the freedom to choose your own attitude, in any given set of circumstances, to what is happening to you and to the people with whom you are in contact.*

It is this inner, subjective, 'existential' freedom that gives man his dignity and worth. It is the quality of courage that enables a person to step into the uncertainty of the unknown as he chooses what and who he himself desires to be.

In this sense, he becomes his own uniqueness. This starts from within the person and not from the manipulation of externals. If we do not exist as persons, and our sense of freedom is an illusion, existence is a mockery. There seems little doubt as to which view enhances human existence, and the work of the counsellor provides evidence that man has an area of real freedom for which he needs to accept responsibility. Counsellors believe that this area can be extended, and the individual helped towards greater self-determination. Here is a further extract from Erich Fromm:

Certainly every psycho-analyst has seen patients who have been able to reverse the trends which seemed to determine their lives, once they became aware of them and made concentrated effort to regain their freedom. But one need not be a psychoanalyst to have this experience. Some of us have had the same experience either with ourselves or with other people: the chain of alleged causality was broken and they took a course which seemed 'miraculous' because it contradicted the most reasonable expectations that could have been formed on the basis of their past performance.[7]

Counselling proves that ordinary people can use their ordinary life experience as stepping stones to personality growth, as a means towards self-development rather than the 'closing of doors'.

A character in an Iris Murdoch novel, answering the question, 'how are you?' replies, 'Dead, otherwise fine'. People die all the time as they live. A wrong decision can destroy a whole world of possibilities. It is possible to close a door in order to feel safe, only to feel less alive. It is fear that makes us close doors, the fear of becoming involved with other people — perhaps of loving too much. Real development in life means conquering that fear, in increasing our willingness and capacity for love. 'We must love one another, or die', wrote W.H. Auden.

Yet love makes us vulnerable by increasing the capacity for pain. 'Look here', says the psychotherapist to Deborah who is angry at what she is seeing and experiencing as she emerges from her psychosis, 'I never promised you a rose garden. I never promised you perfect justice . . . I never promised you peace and happiness. My help is so that you can be free to fight for these things. The only reality I offer you is a challenge, and being well is being free to accept it or not at whatever level you are capable. I never promise lies, and the rose-garden world of perfection is a lie . . . and a bore, too!'[8] (Hannah Green, *I never promised you a rose-garden*).

There are some things that just have to be accepted — painful, unjust things. 'Ah', said Madame Guyon, 'if you knew what peace there is in an accepted sorrow'. Well, that is a knowledge difficult to acquire, but there is a deep down feeling in most of us that that is what needs to happen. Counselling is involved in that quest. It does not offer perfection, just a fighting chance.

References

1. Felix Biestek, *The Casework Relationship*, Unwin University Books, 1961, p.81.
2. Biestek, op. cit., p.123.
3. J.S. Norell, *Ethical Standards of Counselling*, British Association for Counselling, Bedford Square Press of the National Council for Voluntary Organisations, 1974, p.35.
4. J.D. Sutherland, *Some reflections on the development of counselling services*, National Council of Social Service, (now the National Council for Voluntary Organisations) 1971, p.13.
5. Erich Fromm, *The Heart of Man*, Routledge & Kegan Paul, 1964, p.127.

6. The text of this debate was published in *Science* 1956, pp.1057–1066. See also Carl Roger's *On Becoming a Person*, Constable, 1961, pp.363–383.
7. Fromm, op. cit., p.127.
8 Hannah Green, *I never promised you a rose garden*, Pan Books, 1967, p.101.

6   The Relationship and its Structure

Let us first of all imagine an individual wondering whether or not to seek counselling help. He will not take the first step until his stress and anxiety outweighs his fear of what seeking help entails. At this point he will actually start looking round for the most suitable counselling agency. The very diversity might constitute a problem.

Nowadays there are services for a wide range of problems. There are counsellors who specialise in marital and sexual problems; career and educational problems; alcohol and drug dependency problems; work and redundancy problems; personal and bereavement problems.

Our would-be client may not be able to identify his problem in such a way as to give direction to his immediate quest. His problem may seem vague, elusive, indistinct. This may be because his problem is himself, and he has been living with himself all his life.

But he has a right to 'shop around' for the kind of counselling he feels he needs. The alternatives may seem confusing, but they should engender hope. Even if he makes a false start, he can always move elsewhere.

He needs to know that meeting with a counsellor does not place him under any obligation to continue. At the initial meeting both he and the counsellor will be assessing the situation in order to come to a decision. Questions of time, place, fees, and the possible duration (although usually this will be fairly open-ended) need consideration. The counsellor will seek to make clear what he feels he can offer, giving some explanation as to how he works. The client will need to make some commitment and accept responsibility for being an active working partner in the work to be undertaken. Both have the right to be respected by the other as responsible people engaged in an important and worthwhile task.

Even in the assessment interview it needs to be recognised that the basic need, the main source of anxiety, may not emerge until later on, perhaps during the third or fourth session. The client is bound to feel his way cautiously, testing out the counsellor until he feels sufficiently safe in the relationship to venture into the troubled, painful areas.

What does every client bring with him into counselling?

He brings his total past, for the present is the past up-to-date. Much of his personal past will need to be disclosed and explored according to his needs.

He brings the immediate problem that has pressurised him into seeking help.

He brings a certain degree of motivation that may fluctuate disturbingly, and may even disappear altogether.

He brings certain expectations. These, too, may ebb and flow and need to be kept alive. On the other hand, they may be unrealistic and need to be brought down to earth. There are no magic solutions.

He brings his feelings of uncertainty, anxiety, suspicion, despair.

He brings his inner defences. These have enabled him to function so far and, naturally, he is going to be reluctant to lower them.

And what does the counsellor bring?

He brings everything that the client brings: his personal history, his present problems, his fluctuating motivation, his expectations, his feelings, his inner defences. Counsellor and client share a common humanity, and it will be the degree of overlap between them that will be important in the work that lies ahead.

But what else does he bring?

He brings his self-awareness that, hopefully, the new counselling relationship will increase.

He brings his experience of other clients. This should be of great value, but can get in the way by minimizing the uniqueness of the new client before him.

He brings his professional knowledge of human development, but will be wise enough to recognise that this does not automatically turn him into an effective therapist.

He brings his techniques, and these may be important but never all-important.

He brings his ability to communicate, which must be placed at the client's disposal.

He brings his concern for troubled people which was why he became a counsellor in the first place.

He brings his philosophy of life, which includes a particular view of man. At the very least, this is bound to be humanist and positive, and may go beyond this to a form of religious humanism. One thing he must never lose sight of is the fact that the client's viewpoint may be quite different from his own. So he must start where the client is, and respect his terms of reference throughout, especially when they are different.

THE INTAKE PROCESS

The counsellor must try to start every new relationship with a completely open mind. He is going to enter into the life situation of his client in a unique way, learning a great deal of his inner and outer life, his home and marriage, his situation, his range of relationships, his hobbies and leisure pursuits. The counsellor must beware of his own presuppositions.

The client is laying claim to the counsellor's experience, and any speedy hypothesis may close him up. People are capable of reflection in differing degrees, and without the ability to reflect, the counselling cannot even begin. The crisis that has brought the client may have increased the difficulty here, the intensity of the feelings making reflection well-nigh impossible.

Setting the client at ease is the counsellor's first task. Most counselling today claims to be mainly non-directive, but this approach may not initally contribute the necessary warmth that the client needs to feel before he can begin the unburdening that is essential.

This is not to justify the completely directive approach, because that can be experienced as threatening. The ideal is to be sufficiently responsive to the particular need of this unique person as to enable him to begin the sharing process with as little emotional discomfort as possible.

In the first interview — apart from deciding whether the client and counsellor can, in fact, work together — the initial task is to seek to define and establish what is called 'the contract'. This is a mutual undertaking. Each needs to see clearly the nature and the extent of the work on which they are embarking.

Some clients are quite definite in limiting what they are hoping for. It may be they are simply concerned with how they can be helped to function better in a precise area of their lives.

> Edna suffered from a mild form of agorophobia. On a bus, particularly in a traffic jam when going away from home, she would get into a panic. She knew there were deep reasons for this — for there is no effect without cause — but she did not feel equal to the task of seeking those reasons, or was not willing for the protracted self-exploration this might entail. All she wanted was to be helped to handle the symptoms.
>
> John sought help because he was afraid he had become impotent. Behind him was a broken marriage, after which he had become depressed. Eventually he began to function normally at work and socially, but when he became friendly with an attractive young woman, he found he had no sexual feelings for her. He concluded that this meant impotence. The counselling he needed was quite brief. Shocked by his broken marriage, he was fearful of feeling strongly again. He dare not risk a repetition of painful disaster. He was aware of many other areas of his life that needed exploration, but limited his counselling experience to the removal of his sexual fears.

Other clients come not so much with specific symptoms that are troubling them, but a concern about the nature and quality of their relationships with family, friends and colleagues. This, too, although of great importance, can be a limiting of the help counselling can offer.

If this is the initial contract, it will mean a study of the complex relationships the client shared as a child, in the main his relationships within the family circle. The theory here — known technically as 'the object relation theory' — is that we develop our view of ourselves and our environment from the significant persons surrounding us in childhood.

A question always in the counsellor's mind is, to what extent and in what ways is the client's early experience (especially in relationships) affecting, perhaps clouding, his inner feelings and outer judgments in the present. A study at the emotional level of the disturbed relations in the here and now, and tracing them back to their origins in early childhood, can enable a gradual, inner reorganisation of the personality to take place.

Very often the client will unconsciously reproduce patterns of his object relations with the counsellor, so that the actual problem is experienced within the counselling relationship. This kind of first-hand knowledge is invaluable. The client comes to see how he projects his inner world into his outer world wherever he goes.

> James, a quiet, courteous professional man in his 50s, arrived fifteen minutes late for his therapy session. After profuse apologies and lengthy explanations

about a motor-way accident which had caused general delay, he tried to settle down. But his anxiety was obvious. The counsellor asked if punctuality was of special importance to him. Unexpectedly, James exploded harshly. 'This is the first time I have ever been late, and you have to rub it in like that'. The counsellor sat quietly, as did James, head in hands. After what seemed a long time (but was, in fact, not more than a minute) James looked up and said, 'I'm sorry. Your question catapulted me back into childhood. My father — a military man — was a tyrant with regard to time-keeping. If we children were half a minute late for a meal, we had to go without it altogether. If we came in at night a minute later than he had stipulated, we were beaten, right up to the night before leaving for university. I lived in constant anxiety. It was hell, and I'm still dogged by it, even though my father has been dead for seven years.'

It is clear that this second type of contract is likely to lead to a longer counselling relationship than the former, but both of these kinds of contract are likely to point to a deeper need, to some kind of basic personality problem, perhaps that of arrested ego-development. This treatment at the deepest level is necessarily prolonged. It may be beyond the competence of many counsellors — needing extensive psychotherapy. Under these circumstances, the counsellor will refer the client elsewhere.

R.H. Cawley delineates nine levels of psychotherapy which he calls the outer levels (support and counselling), numbers 1, 2, & 3; the intermediate levels, numbers 3, 4, & 5; and the deeper levels (exploration and analysis) numbers 5, 6, 7, 8 & 9. The levels are:

1. unburdening of problems to sympathetic listener.
2. ventilation of feelings within supportive relationship.
3. discussion of current problems with non-judgmental helper.
4. clarification of problems, their nature and origins, within deepening relationship.
5. confrontation of defences.
6. interpretation of unconscious motives and transference phenomena.
7. repetition, remembering, and reconstruction of past.
8. regression to less adult and less rational functioning.
9. resolution of conflicts by re-experiencing and working them through.[1]

Note that number 3 comes into both the outer and intermediate levels, and number 5 into both the intermediate and deeper levels. Brown and Pedder[2] say that it would be more appropriate to speak, not of supportive psychotherapy (the outer level), but of non-exploratory therapy, recognising that this may be a phase that could lead on to deeper levels where the client is 'ripe for judicious exploration'.

It needs to be made clear that it is always the client who decides the level at which he wishes the counsellor to operate. The counsellor may, because of his knowledge and experience, feel it would be advisable in some instances to go deeper than the client desires, but brings no pressure to bear to this end.

The first interview must be seen as laying the foundation stone of confidence on which a steady edifice can be built. The counsellor would be wise to heed two words of warning:

1. The 'presenting symptom' may not indicate the real problem. A client may say 'I'm worried about my daughter', and that could be a genuine worry, but he/she may be saying 'I'm worried about myself'. Certain questions must always be at the back of the counsellor's mind, particularly in the early stages: Is what he/she is talking about what is really bothering him/her? Am I dealing with one problem or two? Does he/she know why he/she has come?

2. Too early reassurance may make it difficult for the client to correct some of his early statements. In the first interview Peter said he loved his father; in the second he admitted he did not get on with his father; in the third said he was afraid of his father; and in the fourth that he hated his father. If Peter's first statement had received the whole-hearted approval of the counsellor, he may have found it impossible to bring out his negative feelings.

The establishing of confidence is of the essence, and this should begin during the intake process.

THE DEVELOPING RELATIONSHIP

Following the introductory phase and the establishing of the contract, the counsellor will seek to encourage the active engagement of the client in the developing process. He would not be human if he did not ask himself, 'What have I on my hands?', but will not yield to the temptation to suppose that his tentative diagnosis is likely to be the whole truth. Any hypothesis needs to be fluid, and the counsellor must be ready to change it altogether.

He is likely to proceed by seeking to identify the immediate precipitating cause and to estimate the strength of his client's motivation, for much will depend on this. He needs to know if the problem is a new one, or of long standing; if the client has talked to anyone else, and if so, in what way he found it useful, or not. He will be alert in regard to any medical factors that could be significant, and suggest a visit to the doctor if this is deemed advisable. If the client has been elsewhere for counselling he will want to know why that terminated. (It is sometimes necessary to suggest a return to a former counsellor, because some clients opt out of counselling when the going gets a little hard, and this may be a pattern that needs breaking.)

It is usually advisable to enquire about self-destructive feelings. Is the client a potential suicide? This does not mean asking bluntly whether he has thought of killing himself, but approaching the matter obliquely with such a question as, 'Have you been tempted to think there's no point in going on?' The response to such a question can be both interesting and revealing.

Having identified the particular problem or area of need, it is usually necessary for the counsellor to elicit and assimilate something of the client's personal history. He will want to know whether the father and mother are still living, and if not, when they died. What of brothers and sisters? What is the client's place in the family? How much present contact is there with members of his primary family. Details of his present working situation. Then, if the client is married, how long for, and whether his partner knows he is seeking counselling help. Are there any children of the marriage? Details of ages and gender.

Most of these facts emerge quickly and naturally. It is not a matter of getting the client to answer a whole range of questions. The counsellor will pick up all he can as the session proceeds, and then ask for gaps in information to be filled. Even if some of this information may seem irrelevant to the client, it helps him to see that whatever his difficulties, these are not seen as the whole truth about him.

At this stage the client may begin to flounder as to how to proceed. He may not know how to organise his material. Why should he? This is a new experience for him. Ideally, this phase should be non-directive, but he can be encouraged to ask for help if he feels need of it. The counsellor may have to direct the client to particular areas that appear important.

Everyone needs to have a better understanding of his own childhood. Our basic attitudes are fairly well established by the age of six or seven, and many people go through life without ever questioning the rightness or validity of them. We spend our first five years introjecting our parents — for better or for worse — establishing our own superego. An important part of counselling lies in helping the client to understand this process.

The client's attitude to his parents is unlikely to be sufficiently objective. Counsellors must proceed gently when exploring this. The parents of most clients will be at least middle-aged and probably quite elderly. To undermine respect for them would be a serious thing to do, yet a client may need to get free of them. No adult should identify too closely with his parents. He needs to retrieve himself; to become his own man.

Eliciting negative feelings about parents should be pursued with delicacy. It is better to approach the matter side-on rather than head-on. Such questions as these are useful: 'Did you feel closer to one parent than the other?' 'Why'? 'If you could have changed the situation at home when you were a child, what changes would you have made?' 'Why?' The answers to such questions may reveal subtle areas of conflict, fears and doubts.

Successful counselling means getting tuned-in to the fruitful areas of exploration. It is not only what the client says, but how he says it. Watching carefully as a client describes a situation can be intriguing. Is the expression appropriate to what is being said?

'Dad used to beat me good and proper', says the forty-year old man with a laugh. The laugh is not genuine. It is inappropriate. He didn't laugh when he was being beaten. He is defending himself from the pain of the memory, and for memories to be healed they need to be re-experienced, not simply recalled.

The family constellation during the first five years is crucial. Then follows all the adjustments necessitated by schooling, when parents are no longer seen as omnipotent and omniscient, and other authority figures become part of the growing child's awareness. At school a child's image of himself may be confirmed, but it can also be challenged. This can lead to anxiety and uncertainty. Feelings of inadequacy experienced in the home may be reinforced in the new situation, and perhaps unfamiliar feelings engendered. On the other hand, success at school may modify earlier feelings of inadequacy.

The importance of the family may recede, and the peer group take its place. As the years pass the attitudes and standards of contemporaries often take precedence over those of the home. These changes often give rise to friction of varying intensity. The contrast between life within the family and life outside is a useful area of exploration. Attitudes and feelings about leaving school may be important.

Then there is the question of social adjustment. Here again the early family situation could be important. Did the client come from a large family? Was there much family interaction? Were there many or few visitors coming into the home? Did his parents choose his friends for him? Were his friends welcome when they called?

We all have social needs and can, therefore, suffer from social deprivation. How a person handles and seeks to satisfy those needs make a significant difference to the way he feels about life generally. So, the groups a client belonged to as a child may still be determining the range of social contacts in the present, and how he is actually relating.

The work area of a client's life needs to be examined. When did his formal education end? Did he go to college or university? An individual's first job may be significant; certainly his adjustment to it is always important. Ideally, school is organised for the sake of the child: the workaday world is only partially arranged with the employee in mind. At work personal factors tend to come second to the work objectives, whether this is the production of goods or even the care of other people. It is surprising the way in which some of the caring organisations fail to care adequately for their own personnel. A 'cog in the machine' feeling can easily intensify into paranoia.

Why did a client choose his particular kind of work or vocation? What does it say about him as a person? Undoubtedly certain temperaments are suited to some tasks, so is he suited? Did he, in fact, have any choice? Perhaps he had to take any job that happened to be available at that time, and then never had the opportunity or courage to change course. Or it could be that his parents wrote his life-script for him and he either did not realise this or lacked the courage to tear it up and write his own.

What is his present attitude to work? Is he apathetic, or driving himself too hard? If the latter, why? For the sake of advancement, or money, or because he is not happy at home? What will his overworking do to him? Is he an 'ulcer type'?

Everyone needs relationships and places where his own idiosyncratic existence is recognised, where his individual identity can be validated, where he enjoys a sense of relatedness, where he feels fully human. It is the lack of this experience of being valued that creates a feeling of depletion deep down within the person. It is this lack, this hunger, that counselling can in some measure hope to satisfy.

The foregoing indicates some of the areas that may need to be looked at, and some of the basic information the counsellor may need to acquire. This is not a comprehensive delineation by any means, but a generalised indication of what might be required as the basis of a counselling relationship of medium duration. No relationship proceeds on strict methodical lines. Factual information is interwoven with emotional/digression and the counsellor knows the importance of staying with significant feelings.

What is the counsellor looking for? What is he hoping will happen? He does not always know. There is a process of elucidation that is intuitive, but part of this is also technical. There needs to be a combination of the two.

How does this person see himself, and why? Is there a lack of congruity, a gap between what he is and how he perceives himself? How can he best be helped towards a more appropriate estimate of himself? Mainly in two ways. Firstly, by the interpretive approach; helping him towards some insight into his own distorted view of himself. And secondly, by the way in which the counsellor treats him. Both are important, and it is the complex interaction between them that can prove valuable.

The way interpretations are made needs watching. They may be made by way of suggestion, or simply by putting known facts together in a way — a different way — that makes just that little bit more sense. In fact, making sense of experience is very largely what counselling is about. This means being emotionally — and not just factually — in touch with all the material the client shares. The need for counselling usually arises because the client's feelings have been hurt. He may come, habitually, to deny his feelings, or to feel ashamed of them because they are so painful. He needs to learn that feelings are not bad. As children, many are taught to distrust their feelings. They are often told they should not feel like that! This is both ridiculous and damaging, and can establish an ambivalent attitude to the whole emotional side of life. The counsellor validates feelings.

What have been and what are the client's basic threats? Of what is he afraid? Are these threats real or imaginary? How does he handle the anxiety which arises? Is there a characteristic way? What have these threats done to him as a person? In view of his personal history, how can he be helped towards creativity and maturity? How have significant people in his life, and significant events, contributed to and interacted with his basic personality structure?

This is a part of a whole range of questions that the counsellor may well ask himself in relation to the client. He will want to discover ways in which he can interact that will be healthful and conducive to growth and development.

Throughout the relationship the counsellor is hoping to elicit insight. We get most satisfaction from what we ourselves discover. Simply to be told something about ourselves can be deflating. Counsellors must believe in the profound possibility of insight, and recognise its value as an experience. Insight releases something we all need, ego-satisfaction — the feeling of 'Eureka, I've found it.'

There is no guaranteed way of encouraging insight, although it usually follows a process of (1) having faced the difficult contemporary situation, (2) having to some extent worked through the negative feelings related to the situation, (3) having learned to live more satisfactorily with the ambivalent feelings engendered by the situation, and (4) finding ways of utilising more positive feelings that have started coming to life.

Leaving a person with insights for which he has found no practical application is not at all satisfactory. A person's awareness may have been heightened, but that is all. The old thought patterns and behaviour patterns remain. So insight may be followed by a high degree of frustration. After all, what is the point of seeing things if essentially there has been no change?

The client must not be left at the insight stage. He will still be controlled by his habitual responses, and bitter disappointment might result. He cannot rely on the magic of the insight. In that way lies disillusionment. In seeking to relate the insight to actual living there should be a progression. First of all *the client feels that things look different*, but the habit of a lifetime fogs things up. So, secondly, he should begin to recognise the meaning of his contemporary experience, *immediately after the habitual pattern of behaviour has manifested itself.*

Then, thirdly, he should begin to look ahead in order to anticipate the kind of event that traps him into his conditioned response. In doing this he can, by being on the alert and therefore ready for the challenge, *begin to modify his behaviour.* He has the insight, but also ability to look ahead, to prepare for the emergency. He can see that other alternatives are open to him and so make an inner preparation before the outer behaviour becomes necessary. In this way the insight will gradually become incorporated into a new pattern of life, with all the satisfaction this can bring.

Another way in which insight can be used is in relating it to other areas of life. Suppose a client sees that his view and attitude towards authority has been conditioned by his relationship with his father as a child, he will then be encouraged to look at how this affected his relationships to authority figures first of all at school, then later in work and vocational situations. A single insight can have many applications.

TERMINATING THE RELATIONSHIP

Following the establishing of the contract in the initial phase, the actual counselling relationship contains many overlapping ingredients, as we have seen. There is the collating of historical material, the actual working through the various problem areas; hopefully there is the welcoming of insight, then the assimilating of the insight into a new established pattern of life, and applying it to other areas.

Gradually, *very* gradually if the relationship has been a long one, consideration must be given to the matter of ending the relationship altogether. The usual procedure is to move from once a week to every two weeks; then perhaps three weeks. The actual end must come at the right moment, which is when the client is ready and able to let go his dependency on the counsellor. Feelings need to be resolved, and the implications of the relationship faced. Louis Marteau writes:

> The counsellor will always see that his endeavour is directed towards the termination of the professional relationship and to the client's maturing ability to regain his personal independence. He will terminate the relationship when the client has ceased to benefit from it or when effective help needed calls for more expertise and/or time than the counsellor can give. The counsellor should realise that though there may be a stage of dependence through which the client has to pass, this should not be maintained longer than is called for by the client's needs, and positive efforts should be made to bring about the situation when the client can use his own resources to the full.[3]

Where the relationship comes to a natural end, and there is no question of referring the client to another therapist or agency, it is as well to suggest that the door is never completely closed. Just as a patient can call upon his doctor's services, so the client may need to know that, should there be further need, he can return.

Gillian came for many months in order to explore the unsatisfactory nature of her marriage relationship. She began to understand the ways in which her earlier infidelity had had a deleterious effect. She discovered resources that enabled her to relate to her husband at the level most satisfactory for him. She had to settle for the 'good enough' marriage. The counselling relationship ended.

Two years later her mother died and the grief of bereavement was too much for her to bear alone. She returned for a few weeks of supportive counselling. Eighteen months later her elder sister died and, at the same time her son was getting married and moving well away from the district. Once again she came for a fairly brief period of counselling.

It is music in the ears of a counsellor when a client says, 'Thank you very much for everything. I can now manage without you.' That is his reward. It is the end to which he is always working.

Even when the counsellor is completely happy at the termination, there is value in suggesting that a client return in six months time just to report progress. If the client agrees, a firm appointment should be made.

Perhaps something should be said about premature terminations. Some clients, having made a second appointment, fail to keep it, giving no explanation at all. This is disturbing to the counsellor. He cannot and should not, and in practice does not 'chase' his clients. He simply has to accept the situation.

Some clients come for a few weeks, but when they get into the work phase of the relationship, they withdraw. This, too, is both annoying and disappointing to the counsellor. It does him no good to blame only himself, by accepting total responsibility for the termination. But he would be wise to be curious about it, and to discuss such cases with his supervisor.

EGAN'S DEVELOPMENTAL MODEL

In counselling it is possible to have too little structure or too much. It is obviously a mistake to force an arbitrary structure on the relationship, which should flow and develop in a natural way. But a structure *in the counsellor's mind* can be very useful. It can save him from losing his way, acting as a kind of map.

Gerard Egan's[4] developmental model is becoming widely known and used. It is not stated in the book, but Egan says it is designed for a short-term counselling relationship covering a ten week period.

After the initial phase, in which the counsellor's goal is to attend completely to the client, there are three further stages. In *stage 1* the counsellor's goal is to respond to the client's story, to establish rapport, and facilitate the client's self-exploration. The client's goal is to explore his experiences in order to discover ways in which he is living ineffectively.

In *stage 2* the counsellor's goal is interpretive understanding, the bringing together of the data, and helping the client to see the behaviour patterns and also the 'larger picture'. The client's goal is dynamic self-understanding.

In *stage 3*, the counsellor's goal is to facilitate action by 'identifying objectives, specifying procedures and assessing behaviour change.' The client's goal is action.

This structure would seem to encourage a fair amount of directiveness in the counsellor which is often the case in comparatively short-term counselling relationships. But here again, it is extremely useful in helping the counsellor to see where he himself and the client are in the relationship, and there is no need for any structure to strangle it.

TRANSFERENCE AND COUNTER-TRANSFERENCE

Every counselling relationship of any importance and significance involves a process known as transference. It can be variously defined but basically it refers to the emotional relationship which inevitably develops between counsellor and client which comes from the emotional attitudes left over from childhood, but now transferred (hence the use of the word 'transference') to the current situation. We all carry over into adult life some unresolved 'left-over' business from childhood which may become operative at any time. The counselling relationship, because it has to do largely with the exploration of childhood experience, is bound to be a situation that encourages its operation.
    We can test out this phenomenon in our everyday life.

Peggy was having a bad time relating — or rather not relating — to her immediate boss. Week after week she spoke of 'unnecessary' friction between them that was making life impossible. She considered asking for a change of department within the organisation where she worked. Peggy was asked whether her boss reminded her of anyone in her past life. After a while she said, 'I haven't seen it before, but she is like one of my sisters; the one I've never related to very well.' Asked what she wanted to say to her sister, not her boss, she exploded, 'Why don't you get off my back.' Later on she smiled and said, 'That's what I want to say to my boss, too'.
Fortunately, the recognition of where the strength of feeling was coming from, eased the stress of the present work relationship. 'After all,' she said, 'my boss can't be blamed because she happens to be like my sister.'

Another area where the transference phenomenon often operates is in the doctor/patient relationship. A man may relate to his doctor in an adult/adult way in a social situation, or when approaching him with a minor ailment that is not undermining him. But should that same man be very ill and the doctor called to him, he may well regress to childhood and transfer his feelings of dependence that, as a sick child, he felt towards his mother. There is a whole range of relationships that can be distorted by the phenomenon called 'transference'.
    This means that during the counselling relationship the client may be reacting to the therapist in a way similar to how he related to a significant person, or persons, from his past, especially his childhood. This is usually happening most strongly following the intake process when the establishing of emotional closeness is a necessary and right development in the relationship.
    The counsellor needs to understand, or at least to question, what is happening at any given moment in relation to the total process. The client will not have his awareness of the importance of what is going on. He may be pre-occupied with his feelings, not understanding their meaning. So an important question that the counsellor must ask *himself*, is 'Where is the client in the process?'

Transference is very often a tool the therapist uses for the understanding and then investigating the forgotten and repressed past.

Breuer worked closely with Freud over many years and is reported to have said of the idea of transference, 'I believe this is the most important thing that we have to make known to the world.' Both W.R.D. Fairbairn[5] and E. Jones[6] tell of the relationship that developed between Breuer and Anna O., one of his patients, with whose treatment Freud was also involved. Breuer knew that what was happening between them *belonged elsewhere*. He lived with this for a while, but as the treatment was nearing its end, she began to have erotic feelings, which alarmed Breuer. He withdrew from any further explorations in this threatening area and, according to rumour, took his wife on a second honeymoon for the sake of mutual reassurance.

Early on, Freud called transference a 'false connection', seeing it as a departure from the process of true analysis, but changed his mind, finding it an invaluable tool.

This does not mean that only positive, 'loving' feelings are brought into the relationship. Very often it is the harsh, negative feelings that — very usefully — come to life. 'You sound just like my father', is a statement that could provide an important clue, and point towards an area for useful exploration.

Obviously, it is more often than not the mother/child and/or father/child relationship that is being relived in a certain form in the counselling room. The sex of the counsellor is unimportant: a man counsellor may elicit the emotions associated with the mother/child relationship, whereas a woman counsellor can call forth elements of the father/child relationship.

It is clear that with transference we are dealing with *unconscious* factors. Some counselling seeks to keep everything within the conscious area, and to take no cognisance of transference. The Marriage Guidance Movement encourage this approach, and Carl Rogers has argued this case as regard to his client-centred emphases. He maintains that in using this approach the counsellor acts simply as a facilitator, makes no interpretations, judgments or evaluation, but seeks only to clarify what the client brings. He was forced to admit that an element of transference occurs 'in a very small minority of cases'[7], and later that 'such attitudes occur in *some* degree in the majority of cases'[8], but he discourages any use being made of it.

Which raises the question as to what use *can* be made of it, not simply as providing clues to be followed, but openly in the counselling process. At one level the fact of it can be simply mentioned, and then left to the client to make such use of it as he may be able. At another level it can be used explicitly and comprehensively to help the client see what he is doing to the relationship and why, and how his other relationships might be affected by the same dynamic factor.

Earlier in this chapter we have written of the termination process, and obviously this must take account of the transference factor. The following is a brief outline of how the transference phenomenon operates. The intensity of it varies in every case, of course.

To start with the counsellor and client are usually unknown to each other, the distance between them is total. The client, experiencing his need of counselling help, and having decided on a particular counsellor, makes the initial contact.

In the early stages of the relationship a bridge is being built between the two

participants. Feelings and attitudes about figures from the past are transferred
from the client to the counsellor. This is one aspect of the psychological
mechanism of projection. The mind of a client can be likened to a cinema film
projector. The picture on the screen is actually out of sight at the back of the
cinema. These projections are unconscious.

When the relationship is well-developed, the projections can be explored at
the emotional level. Before this can take place there needs to be an emotional
alignment between counsellor and client. The counsellor, naturally, is further
ahead than the client in his understanding, and so may have to wait for some
catching up to be done. Transference interpretations can be made too soon,
before the client is ready for them.

With the relationship being established there is a considerable overlap between
counsellor and client. The counsellor may partially then fulfil many roles,
becoming father, mother, teacher, marriage partner, guru in turn. Positive and
negative feelings are around. These projections are a necessary part of the
healing process. The degree to which all these are explored depends upon the
level of the therapeutic relationship. There is here a partial identification, which
should be the limit. There needs to be an objective part of the counsellor outside
the transference, otherwise we have what has been called 'the gruesome twosome'.

During the ending-process, the client is helped to take back into himself his
own projections, to retrieve possession of himself.

There is also a counter-transference phenomenon. In an article in *The British
Journal of Guidance and Counselling*, January 1974, Jock Wilson of Bishop
Otter College, Chichester, wrote:

> It is noticeable that the literature on psychoanalysis contains less about
> counter-transference than about transference. No doubt Freud's early ideas
> of the analyst as a 'mirror' on to whom the patient could project his problems,
> has had an inhibiting effect on writers on counter-transference — a mirror,
> presumably, is not capable of such feelings! But the disparity still exists.
> Winnicott in a chapter supposedly on counter-transference has much more
> to say in it about transference. Likewise Storr in a chapter on 'Transference
> and Counter-transference' devotes seventeen pages to the former and three to
> the latter. Yet for therapy both are equally important.[9]

It is a mistake to imagine that only the client has needs. The counsellor also
has them — he is not a neuter. This means that the counsellor should be in
touch with his own projections and needs, particularly his need to be needed.
So he must watch for any strong negative and/or positive feelings being generated
by the relationship. It seems likely, for instance, that Breuer became scared of
what Anna O's erotic feelings were doing to him, so he felt compelled to cease
work in the transference field. For the counsellor to collude with the client, to
lose his objectivity, could be damaging to the client and render the relationship
ineffective.

Jenny explained in her first session that she had, sometime previously,
withdrawn from a counselling relationship. She was reluctant to give details
or state reasons, but it was obvious from the start that whatever had happened
would get in the way of any useful work being accomplished. Eventually it

emerged that over a period of weeks the transference and counter-transference feelings had got out of hand. She was sexually inexperienced and he, the counsellor, a young married man. Succeeding sessions with him consisted of both of them struggling, unsuccessfully, to control their sexual urges. Intercourse took place, and the 'counselling' sessions became a mere pretext. Mutual guilt well-nigh overwhelmed them. The sessions had to end, as did the relationship itself. For some time Jenny felt she could not take the risk of looking elsewhere for counselling help, but now found she had a double need. There was the initial problem that took her to the previous counsellor, and also the guilt from the disastrous sexual relationship that had resulted. Seeking help she had been sorely damaged. Restoration was slow and painful.

The counsellor should, therefore, be on the alert for any warning signs. If he begins to fear his own emotional involvement with a client, he would do well to consider the way in which he thinks about the relationship prior to the appointment. Any desire to miss the interview is obviously significant, as is the wish to terminate or prolong it.

Writing an introduction to Ferrand and Hunneybunn's *The Caseworker's Use of Relationships* (Tavistock, 1962) John Bowlby writes:

> Transference and counter-transference reactions are the stuff of which the caseworker's daily life is made. Her job is not to avoid them but to learn how best to deal with them, recognising always that the way the client and she treat each other is neither wholly a mere repetition of the past, nor wholly a matter of fact coping with the present, but the result by each of an unconscious appraisal of the present in terms of more or less similar situations that each has experienced in the past. How could it ever be otherwise?[10]

Written for caseworkers, this is equally valid for counsellors.

REFERENCES

1. R.H. Cawley, Association of University Teachers of Psychiatry Newsletter, Jan. 1977.
2. Dennis Brown & Jonathan Pedder, *Introduction to Psychotherapy*, Tavistock, 1979, p.99.
3. Louis Marteau, *Ethical Standards in Counselling*, edited by H.J. Blackham, British Association for Counselling, Bedford Square Press of the National Council for Voluntary Organisations, 1974, p.24.
4. Gerard Egan, *The Skilled Helper*, Brooks/Cole Publishing Co., Monterez, California, 1975.
5. W.R.D. Fairbairn, *Psychoanalytic Studies of the Personality*, Tavistock, 1962.
6. E. Jones, *Sigmund Freud, Life and Work, Vol 1*, Hogarth Press, 1953.
7. Carl Rogers, *Counselling and Psychotherapy*, Boston, Houghton Mifflin, 1951.
8. Carl Rogers, *Client-Centred Therapy*, Boston, Houghton Mifflin, 1951.
9. The Winnicott reference relates to *The Maturational Processes of the*

Facilitating Environment, Hogarth, 1960.

The Storr reference relates to *The Integrity of the Personality*, Penguin Books, 1963.

10. M.L. Ferrand and N.K. Hunneybunn, *The Caseworker's Use of Relationships* Tavistock, 1962, pp.ix-x.

7 Counselling and the Family

This chapter is not simply about marriage counselling, although that will be considered. It has a wider reference altogether. There are those who fear for the future of marriage and the family, and we feel it might be useful for some kind of general assessment to be made.

Perhaps the first thing that needs to be said is that marriage breakdown, with provision for divorce and remarriage, is not a product of the twentieth century. It is a phenomenon to which the ancient law systems of the Babylonians, the Jews, the Greeks, and the Romans bear witness.

One of the impacts of Christianity was the establishing throughout Europe and in those parts of the world where European civilisation has had an influence, of the ideal for marriage as a life-long and indissoluble union. Over the last two hundred years or so, there has been a gradual lessening of Christian influence which has accelerated over the past fifty years. There are those who argue that the church should never have exercised its power so as to impose its own ideals upon the whole citizenship of any country. So, in a sense, earlier solutions to the problem of marriage breakdown have been finding their way back, and this has inevitably created difficulties for all sections of the Christian church. In view of its concept of marriage, how can it come to terms with marital failure? We will not be able to go into all aspects of this intricate and delicate subject as it affects the churches, but much of what follows will have certain implications in this regard.

SOCIOLOGICAL BACKGROUND

From what we know of the most primitive societies up to the more sophisticated contemporary ones, the relationship between men and women has been subject to regulations of various kinds. The primary purpose behind these is the maintenance of social stability, but other facts enter into the matter. There is the need to perpetuate the clan, tribe or nation; the desirability of economic stability; the need for the proper passing of property and wealth from one generation to the next. There are also more personal reasons, such as the perpetuation of a family name.

Societal reasons become entangled with what seems to be instinctive emotional responses to particular forms of sexual conduct. There is, for example, the almost universal abhorrence of incest (sexual relationships between parents and their children, or between brothers and sisters). Freud made the interesting suggestion that society actually came into existence because of the incest barrier, in that man was compelled to form groups larger than the family within which it was possible legitimately to marry.

In addition to the above reasons for the regulating of sexual conduct, there are those that reflect religious belief. The embargo on adultery in the ten commandments (Exodus 20), which had already been set in a religious context by the earlier code of Hammurabi, comes from the nomadic period in Hebrew history when it was necessary to avoid civil strife, and wife-stealing would be bound to lead to blood-shed. It appears as a God-given commandment and set in the context of the Mosaic covenant, but its practical necessity is also obvious.

The regulations reflect the deepseated possessiveness in human nature. This is seen in the commandment related to covetousness, where the male-dominated Hebrew society forbade the coveting of a neighbour's property, before mentioning the neighbour's wife, stock and servants.

Most legal codes seem to recognise that men have greater difficulty than women in the ordering of their sexual habits. The majority of early societies were polygamous. Hebrew society condemned 'sacred prostitution' as a threat to its religious faith and practice, but did not prohibit concubinage and secular prostitution.

There is no anthropological evidence of any society beginning as monogamous and developing towards polygamy, except in the disguised form of divorce and remarriage. (This happened in Rome wherever monogamy was the supposed rule.) The normal development in society seems to have been from polygamy to monogamy, and this usually happened not for moral reasons but under external pressures, such as the inability to buy or maintain more than one wife, or a balancing out of the proportions of men and women within a particular society.

It seems that Hebrew society was polygamous until the period of Greek domination. It was not until the time of Christ that monogamy appears as the norm rather than the exception and this was nearing the end of the Greek period. Rabbinic teaching discouraged, but did not forbid polygamy.

Jesus said that the Mosaic permission for the Jewish male to divorce his wife was a concession to men's hardness of heart, and was not God's will and intention (Mark 10). He quoted the late Hymn of Creation found in Genesis 1 in which God is described as making male and female *together* on the sixth day of creation. Jesus said that maleness and femaleness belong to the nature of God, and a man and woman coming together form one flesh. It is not surprising, then, that Christianity gave such an impetus to monogamistic thinking and practice, so that following the conversion of Constantine the Great (AD274 or 288 to 337) and the establishing of the holy Roman Empire with the identification of state and church, monogamy became the accepted pattern of sexual relationships.

THE CONTEMPORARY SITUATION

Many new factors are contributing to the crisis that is affecting the whole concept of monogamous marriage. It is possible to identify some of these.

First of all there is the fact of increasingly efficient methods of contraception. It is possible for both men and women to have a full sex life with, if they so desire, a number of partners, without the risk of children. Seeing, then, that unwanted children need not be considered, what is the point of marriage? This is the thinking of some.

Secondly, there is the increase in general mobility. Husbands and wives may not feel they belong to any specific community, or may feel they belong to different communities. Commuter-land has little community feel about it. Work can be at a distance. There may be a daily journey of thirty to fifty miles each way — or more. Work may take one partner away for the week so they spend only weekends together. This is far removed from earlier times when a family lived in a relatively small close-knit community, from which there was no escape.

More than all those variations of life-style made possible by our increased mobility, there is the fact that if someone wishes to escape from the established domestic scene altogether, he (or she) can do this more easily than at any previous time in human history.

Thirdly, there is the so-called 'nuclear family' of husband, wife and no more than two children, with no grandparents, aunts, uncles and cousins within easy reach. It is recognised that this can prove very unsatisfactory as a viable unit. Is not the effect of this claustrophobic? Husband and wife may need more than each can provide for the other; they may need fairly regular contact with other family members. The children need contact with more than Mum and Dad; they need to learn to relate to their grandparents' generation. The development of personality seems to require contact with a whole range of diverse persons in a way that the nuclear family cannot easily provide.

The growth of communes is a protest against the insularity of so much of today's family living, but most of these tend to close down within a year or two.

Fourthly, there is that small section of the women's liberation movement which sees marriage and motherhood as demeaning to women. Perhaps we should not be surprised at this admittedly minority development in view of what has been said above of the prevalence of male-dominated societies. We can be grateful that most women claiming their legitimate equality with men are not anti-men. Change needs a healthier motivation than hatred. Those who are so motivated do a great disservice to their cause, and in the process encourage bitterness between the sexes.

Fifthly, there is the waning power of the Christian church in all its forms. The forces of secularism have released people from what many had come to see as a tyranny with accompanying sanctions. In 1975 for the first time in Britain there were more marriages celebrated with a civil ceremony, than a religious one (179,330 as compared with 179,237). This trend, which will continue even though the Anglican Church is changing its stand on the remarriage of divorcees, is explained largely by the rising proportion of marriages involving divorced people. In that year, one in five of those marrying had been divorced.

But that is only one side of the picture. It seems likely that the majority of people in the western world still see the monogamous marriage as desirable and normal. Standards in marriage have undoubtedly changed. Most marriages today provide the chance for a much richer personal development for both partners within the relationship as compared with previous times. The wedding ceremony itself used, in a subtle way, to suggest an inequality between men and women by referring to 'man and wife', as if the man had his identity as a man, but the woman had her identity only by virtue of being a wife!

All that has changed, for which most husbands and wives should be exceedingly grateful. Modern marriage has been 'renovated and considered as a free association between husband and wife'. Marriage is now regarded as a partnership between persons of equal status, in which the roles of husband and wife are fixed only by biological considerations, and not by social conventions that make the man the provider and the woman the home-maker. This means that new patterns and adaptations are necessary. New expectations must be turned into new attitudes, new roles, a new form of relationship.

But few gains are pure gain. Every change, even a change for the better, carries within it its own risk. Jack Dominian points to one such risk in *Marital Breakdown:*

> The fostering of egalitarian relationships between the spouses and children permits bonds which are based on the value of personal worth rather than on the arbitrary basis of fear and authority. These structured hierarchical relationships were undoubtedly restricting but had the advantage of stability, continuity and little need for invention. There is security in conformity. Equality requires constant adaptation so that personal rights and status are safeguarded and feelings not hurt.
>
> To achieve this in the ever-changing complexity of roles within marriage requires personalities who are adaptive, flexible and stable, to accommodate each other without compromise or damage. When these qualities are absent there will be ambiguity, confusion, disappointment, difficulties in communication, and much misunderstanding.[1]

So, there are marriage partners of both sexes who need the dominating strength of their partners in order to feel secure enough to function. This may be seen and criticised as neurotic, but it cannot be ignored that there are those for whom marriage never will be or can be a partnership of equals.

The prevalence of divorce is not only disturbing to religious people for whom marriage is a life-long sacrament, but it rightly concerns those anxious about social stability. The real problem is not the divorce rate but the marriage breakdown rate. The increase in the divorce rate is due to law reform, but this only brought to light the extent of marriage breakdown. The percentage of actual breakdowns need not be higher today than previously. The difference now is that divorce is more of a possibility. In earlier times people had to live with the breakdown or take the considerable risk of unofficial separation. There is evidence that with the common-law unions which were widespread in mid-nineteenth century England, there were many breakdowns, so perhaps things are not very different. It can be argued that it is more honest to admit to the failure of a marriage, and divorce the only positive course to follow. The view that people should continue to live together for the sake of the children when the death of their mutual love is resulting in behaviour damaging to all within the family circle, is hardly a moral one.

The fact that two-thirds to three-quarters of divorcees marry again shows that they are not opposed to marriage itself, but to a particular union that for some reason proved too painful to endure.

A great deal depends on what is meant by the word 'marriage'. Is it seen as a man and a woman living together subsequent to a civil or religious wedding ceremony? Or is it to be seen as a certain quality of relationship?

Let it be admitted that a marriage ceremony is no guarantee of a lasting, loving relationship, which must come from commitment at depth. It seems likely that we are going to see many monogamous relationships without 'benefit of clergy' or registrar. Many non-believers recognise that the concept of one man, one woman joined together for life is not an arbitrary one. It can be a strong, deep and attractive experience. Such a union offers the possibility of the full development of the affections, understanding and security men and women need. The nature of men and women is such that this can open the door to great happiness and fulfilment. Church ministers are finding that many couples who have been living together for a number of years are deciding to marry after all. G.K. Chesterton used to say that 'free love' is a contradiction in terms, in that it is in the nature of love to bind people together creatively.

It is sometimes said that in the U.S.A. there is developing what may be called hidden polygamy, i.e. the idea of successive marriages: a trial marriage, a child-rearing marriage, and a companionate marriage. In some instances there may be two marriages — with the first or second or the second and third. Seeing most American products are exported, presumably this is something the rest of the western world can expect to happen there. It is our opinion that this idea will be implemented by only a minority of the population.

It is a myth that more couples who marry young get divorced. The statistics of all marriages show a peak of marital breakdown in the early years, but this peak is the same irrespective of age. It is because of the volume of young marriages that it seems theirs is at greater risk.

It is only under very unusual circumstances that marriages of less than three years duration terminate, so it is not surprising that at this point there is a peak. There are other peaks as well. One of these comes at twenty to twenty-five years, when the children are grown and leaving home; the wife may be nearing the menopause, and the couple — having endured the generation gap in relation to the children — now face the 'spouse gap'. It is not only newly-weds who stand in need of help. Many in their forties and fifties find themselves in a desperate plight.

Marriage remains a significant social institution. The welfare of societies and nations depends to a great extent on the state of the individual marriage and family. No society can afford to leave sexual relationships and the processes of procreation entirely unregulated. We must learn how best the rights of the individual can be reconciled with the needs of society. Modern marriages seem to be committed to the goal of freedom and independence, and to the attainment of the greatest possible personal fulfilment. This is commendable. But there is another fact that has to be kept in mind. No acceptable alternative to the family that is based on husband-wife-children has been devised for the emotional growth and development, and the socialisation of children.

Seeing, then, that there seems no alternative to the family, two things need to be accomplished. Firstly, there should be wide-spread education and preparation for marriage. Secondly, there should be the provision of readily available and effective help for those whose marriages are in jeopardy. The rest of this chapter will be devoted to these important matters.

PREPARATION FOR MARRIAGE

Ignorance may be bliss in certain areas of life, but marriage is not one of them. It is easy to assume these days that all young people know what they need to know in order to enter the married state. There is certainly much more sexual knowledge around, but even here it is often surprising to discover vast tracts of ignorance, and other large areas of *mis*-information. The young people themselves may feel their knowledge is adequate, when in fact it is woefully deficient.

One major problem is the question as to who should prepare people for marriage. What has been learned at school about human relationships and the birds and bees is too far back for many. Parents cannot in general be relied upon. Church ministers may say a few words to couples they join in holy wedlock, but that is likely to be somewhat superficial, and certainly inadequate. In any case, less than half of weddings now take place in church.

This is a thorny problem indeed. Some churches are taking up the challenge and doing much more in preparatory work, but in the main this reaches only their own membership. Youth clubs could accept more responsibility, but overall their numbers are few. Perhaps local authorities should set up regular courses on the subject at evening institutes. The Marriage Guidance Movement is active in this field.

It has been said that when a couple decide that they want to marry there are, in fact, six people concerned. First, there is the couple as they are. Secondly, there is the couple as each thinks the other to be. Thirdly, there is the couple as each thinks himself or herself to be.

The last four are in part the product of what the psychologists call projection and fantasy. If the subsequent marriage is to have a chance of being a happy one, two requirements are needful. In the first place, those projections that falsify each prospective marriage partner's view of the other, and the fantasies that have no foundation in reality, need to be worked through. In other words each, ideally, should gain a reasonably accurate picture of the other and of himself or herself, for only on the basis of reality can mutual understanding be reached.

It is, of course, the function of the engagement period to provide something along this line, though it is rarely possible to complete the process apart from the actual living together in marriage. Nevertheless, properly used, this period can do much to help prepare couples for the adventure that lies ahead. Young people should be taught to anticipate the emotional adjustments necessary in marriage.

Some people marry for insufficient reasons; perhaps to escape from their present pattern of life; for security reasons; for a home of their own; in order to enjoy sex legitimately. The fully sufficient reason is the desire to share a total life with this particular person.

It seems to us that ideally love should be the starting point resulting eventually in sexual fulfilment within the stable relationship of marriage. Many young people today are putting love and sex the other way round. There is no guarantee that a sexual encounter will lead to love. If it is only instinct that brings two people together, love may never be born.

Perhaps this is the place to say something about pre-marital sex. First of all this needs to be differentiated from promiscuity. Obviously there is a promiscuous minority that is problematic to any society. Promiscuity at any age — whether in the teens or forties — is a sign of basic immaturity.

There have been many studies relating to the sexual behaviour of today's young people. These tend to show that one third of young men and one quarter of young women have had sexual intercourse by the age of nineteen, but most of their sexual experience is between couples who intend to get married — even if in a percentage of these this does not happen. So it seems that much pre-marital sexual activity is not, by any means, promiscuous behaviour.

There is evidence that when the promiscuous do marry — and try to settle down — their 'experience' can be more hindrance than help. There appears to be a direct relation between promiscuity before marriage and infidelity in marriage. It seems to be legitimate to argue the case with young people that couples who are to share life together are helped by sharing the sexual learning process, and that this can happen more satisfactorily within the security of marriage commitment. To suggest that sex is not integral to the human personality is false. To suggest that it belongs properly within the marriage bond, rings true.

Ideally the sex act should be the climax of a slowly maturing experience. As the expression of love, sex is enriching and beautiful. To use another human being — even if this is with his or her consent — simply as a means to self-understanding or mutual understanding is a denial of our full humanity.

This consideration of the importance of the sexual should include the recognition that once it has taken place, it can never be undone. The couple are, to some extent, changed people. The sexually aroused woman, in particular, is no longer the same person as before. If the ideal is that marriage should possess a sense of newness, then what must contribute most to this is when the sex act is not already a part of the couple's past experience of each other.

It may seem old-fashioned to advocate 'chastity before marriage and fidelity within marriage' as the guardians of true happiness and lasting pleasure, but only if sex is no longer seen as one of life's most precious gifts. It is the good things that we quite rightly safeguard and value.

Those engaged in pre-marriage counselling know full well that this is not the time or place for lecturing couples approaching the most important choice and commitment they will ever make. There needs to be an atmosphere of informality and relaxation in which they can feel free to talk of whatever concerns them most.

Each can be encouraged to spend time considering two important questions:

1. To what extent am I marriageable to anyone?
2. To what extent are my friend and I compatible i.e. marriageable *to each other*?

Another essential area for exploration is that of the couple's expectations, from each other and from the relationship. How similar or how different are their family backgrounds? Have they an adequate knowledge and understanding of each other's childhood?

The counsellor is not attempting to put his own ideas over to them, but indicating a willingness to share whatever insights and information they may request. He belongs to those who come for counsel. He should permit them to take the lead in the conversation and guide the course of the mutual search for understanding and emotional growth. The values they achieve and the decisions they reach will be their own. They will feel a new sense of responsibility in carrying them out. It is the quality of the relationship offered by the counsellor that opens up the door to emotional growth and understanding.

There is a dynamic character about pre-marital counselling. There should be a going forward together. The counsellor will gently place responsibility upon the couple, that at the outset of their joint life they may learn to show consideration for each other's wishes, and reveal the outgoing nature of love.

Some counsellors think that three interviews are a minimum requirement, two before the wedding and one after the honeymoon; or one individual conference with each person and one combined conference. Some brides-to-be cannot open up to a male counsellor, and some grooms-to-be are inhibited if the counsellor is female. Healthy mature people are those who are learning to live openly instead of hiding secrets and defending against discovery. Certainly self-revelation is an urgent need in marital love, and the counselling hour is most useful when it creates a freedom to be oneself, an atmosphere which facilitates the practice of open expression, and the acceptance of genuine feelings.

An interview after the honeymoon is an excellent time to evaluate the relationship which has begun. It may be that emotional blocks and anxieties need to be worked through because these may arise even at this early stage. A consideration of the next steps of moving forward to a larger fulfilment of marital love is useful at this juncture. Many of the difficulties and tendencies that defeat marital success appear in the first months of the couple's life together. An interview at this time with a trusted counsellor may be decisive for the future.

There is also the fact that after the isolation of the honeymoon, there is the need to establish wider social relationships. It is not healthy for an individual family to rely entirely on itself as a self-sufficient unit.

The counsellor's major responsibility is to place his own knowledge and experience at the disposal of the couple. They are unlikely to have sufficient knowledge of what the marriage tie involves for both parties. They need to learn that the love which gives permanence to marriage is not an emotion but a sentiment i.e. it is an organisation of all the emotions, impulses and ideas around the personality of the other. The wishes of each should be motivated by the other's needs — social, moral, spiritual, physical.

Some of the essential points that may need to be opened up, clarified and defined could include the following:

1. The fact that love can never be merited. Love is always a gift. Neither partner is conferring a privilege upon the other.

2. A happy marriage is an achievement, not a gift. The initial attraction is spontaneous, but the turning of that mutual attraction into a steady, fruitful and growing relationship needs effort and thought. A happy marriage is the fruit of the spirit in which it is entered into.

3. As already suggested, marriage is no longer a social institution merely, but is increasingly seen as a partnership. This relates to the pay-packet and how it is to be spent; to the size and spacing of the family; to how the children are to be reared. Husband and wife are two parts of a complete whole and each is complementary to the other in his or her distinctiveness.

4. Married love should be 'balanced love'. There need be no withdrawing from relationships which were mutual before marriage. Later on there should be no withdrawal of the wife's demonstrated love for her husband when the children arrive. On the other hand, there should not be total absorption in business affairs by the husband. Married love needs time and attention if it is to be kept fresh and lasting. Some unshared interests can be maintained. A deadly enemy of any marriage can be boredom.

5. Turning a blind eye to irritating habits and characteristics. Love is not blind in itself, but it should enable a person to be blind at certain times and in certain particulars. It is amazing how small faults can weaken a reasonably strong relationship. It is also true that shared trouble strengthens a relationship. In marriage undue fault-finding is a habit that should not be allowed to start.

6. The question of in-laws should be thoroughly discussed. Each marriage partner needs to recognise the nature of the emotional ties that the other has with his or her parents. Are those ties childish or mature? Is there likely to be the problem of psychological dependence? These are questions that should be asked, and answers sought quite early on in the relationship. They should not be left until too near the actual marriage.

7. The physical facts. It is astonishing how, even in this so-called permissive age, ignorance regarding the facts of sex still does exist. It is necessary for each to be aware of the needs of the other. They need to know what is and what is not legitimate in this sexual relationship. Sexual adjustment is one of the most important that must be made if the marriage is to be enriching to both partners. The need to integrate sex and love is fundamental.

As young people journey through adolescence to adulthood, an ideal 'other' is slowly being formed within them. They are not putting a particular face or form to the ideal. Then something happens — there may have been a number of friendships of varying importance and intimacy, but here is someone with whom the other can glimpse a total life. There is a shared feeling of belonging together, and increasingly each comes to see in the other his or her own growth towards maturity. Discovery and disclosure go hand-in-hand.

This kind of love is experienced as a gift, but a marriage has to be created out of the raw material of our needs, which include our desire for companionship as well as for sexual fulfilment. Love creates the marriage, but there may be times of stress when the marriage will need to sustain the love. This takes us forward to our next subject: marriage counselling.

MARRIAGE COUNSELLING

Learning to love is a social development and a significant achievement. On the journey through life we accumulate experiences some of which help us towards this development and achievement.

The baby begins by loving himself. As far as he is concerned there is no one else to love. He welcomes whatever satisfies his hunger and comfort without knowing or caring how it reaches him. After some months he manages to separate himself sufficiently from his mother to recognise that she is the one who provides these satisfactions. Later on, father comes into focus as an important person. Then brothers and sisters, grandparents and other relatives take their places in the family constellation. Eventually friends of a similar age are discovered in the play-school, the playground and elsewhere, as well as other people such as teachers.

Along these paths of significant relationships the lessons of love are learned and the developing person discovers the need for, and the satisfaction of, loving people. Not all loves lead to marriage, of course, but every person loved contributes to the individual's ability to become a lover. Without these 'preparatory exercises' in the discovery of love, marriage would have no hope of success. In any case, deficiencies along this perilous route undoubtedly create problems in marriage and sometimes lead to its breakdown.

When considering the major causes of marital breakdown, the failure to communicate with each other must be placed first and foremost.

During the engagement period a couple may have felt there was never sufficient time to share with each other all the things they deemed important yet, after a brief experience of marriage, find themselves with little or nothing to say to each other. This is sad for whatever reason the communication ends. One reason may seem to show consideration — the desire not to worry the partner. In this way, however, anxieties lead to the keeping of secrets, and this inevitably results in a lessening of confidence. Any unshared secret, even if it is entirely 'innocent', establishes an emotional distance and creates a hidden barrier between husband and wife.

There needs to be communication at three levels. There is the ordinary level of sharing the ordinary concerns and happenings of everyday life. Then there is the deeper level involving the sharing of feelings. It is not just a case of 'What has happened today?' but also 'How have you felt about what has happened today?' Tuning-in to each other's world of thought and feeling is the essential kind of sharing, and it is usually the closing down of this area that leads to mutual disappointment and, finally, suspicion and resentment.

Lastly, there is sexual communication. Here we mean the way in which the sex life expresses and develops the feeling of 'one flesh', of belonging together in a unique way. This is an area demanding understanding and tenderness, of knowing what delights the other, and makes the partner aware of what is personally enriching within the sexual relationship.

There are those who believe that if the sexual communication is satisfactory, everything else will follow. Our experience in marriage counselling leads us to believe otherwise. It is more often the failure to relate at the level of shared feelings that is the problem. If that is achieved and maintained, the needed sexual adjustments will usually follow.

The counsellor will seek to help the partner to open up channels of communication. Seeing them individually is important, particularly at the beginning of the counselling relationship, but seeing them together is all-important. It is then that the communication breakdown reveals itself. The focus of attention is the relationship itself, and forcing the couple into direct contact is often fruitful. The counsellor will be careful not to take sides. Support for the wife will be experienced as anti-husband, and vice versa.

What often emerges is the way in which each has fallen into the habit of guessing what the other thinks and feels. There is a story of a married couple who left England for Canada to start a new life. After a while the husband convinced himself that his wife was missing all the relatives and friends back home (which was true) and longed to return (which was false). At the same time the wife was convincing herself that her husband was not happy at work and wanted his old job back (neither of which was true). Thinking they were sacrificing themselves for the other, they agreed to return to England. Mid-way across the Atlantic they discovered the truth that neither of them wanted to return.

So, one of the things the counsellor is always saying is, 'Don't guess. Ask each other, and tell each other.'

Certain questions are worth posing, such as:

1. (a) What does he think? (about in-laws, friendships, etc.)
   (b) What does she think?
2. (a) What does she think he thinks?
   (b) What does he think she thinks?
3. (a) What does he think that she thinks that he thinks?
   (b) What does she think that he thinks that she thinks?

This kind of questioning often produces surprises for both partners.

Because of the breakdown in creative communication, or the failure to achieve this in the first place, it often happens that the only kind of communication that does take place is of a destructive kind. Many find themselves constantly quarrelling, and very often they cannot say where, how and about what the quarrelling began. There is a chain reaction. Some minor disagreement regarding, say, money, can lead on to sex, the children, and end up with the in-laws.

Quite apart from this kind of chain-reaction, quarrels very often follow a particular sequence. It is as though couples make the quarrel into a reasonably safe exercise by establishing a regular pattern which leaves them both with the feeling that, as usual, 'we got through that'.

This kind of quarrelling relationship can develop in a marriage because the couple are unprepared for those necessary and proper differences of opinion. These differences can become useful as growing pains. Some of them will not be resolved, and neither partner has the right to demand submission of the other for the sake of maintaining an uneasy peace.

Quarrels can arise from frustration. There may be a strong desire to communicate without the knowledge of how to proceed. There may be physical reasons for tension i.e. the wife may be suffering from pre-menstrual tension, and the advice here is for her to seek medical help, and the husband to seek the information that will make him more understanding.

Quarrels may be due to personality differences: extrovert versus introvert; radical versus reactionary; cavalier versus puritan; house-proud wife versus untidy husband.

Quarrels can be caused by different approaches to marriage, the partners having been brought up by very different sets of parents. A cartoon caption read: 'There are six people in every marriage bed.' In the bed lay husband and wife. On the wall behind the husband were pictures of his mother and father. On the wall behind the wife were pictures of her parents. Here the task is to define the differences and discover the reasons for them.

While most counselling concentrates on the inner factors, the wise counsellor will recognise that there could be external factors making life very difficult for the couple, such as inadequate housing, financial worries, difficulties caused by the work situation, practical things going wrong continually. These external stresses may not be the whole truth, or even the most important part of it, but they should not be overlooked.

In the early years of marriage, particularly when the children are small, a couple can become very tired, quite apart from the inevitable anxiety accompanying the responsibilities of parenthood. The counsellor can sometimes help a couple to see that it is exhaustion rather than waning affection that is causing them to quarrel. It needs to be recognised that the human mind is unable to bear more than a certain amount of anxiety and when that point is reached it is projected outwards, often on to the marriage partner.

There is comfort in the thought that it is easier to off-load on to those we love, and who love us, than on to others with whom there is no close, sustaining relationship. Those who do not love us would not stand it. Having said this, however, it is as well to remember that our loved ones also have their limits. They, too, can stand only so much. Their love for us must not be exploited or taken for granted.

Jealousy is a major cause for much bitter quarrelling. Both husband and wife need to understand that jealousy is a natural reaction in certain situations. Here again it is communication that can ease matters.

That some marriages need to be more 'open' than they are, allowing 'spaces' in the 'togetherness' of the partners, is undoubtedly the case. But the idea of 'perfect sexual freedom', each partner allowing the other extra-marital liaisons, or periods of partner-swapping between friends and acquaintances, seems to us unwise and dangerous. It is a denial of primary needs; the need for a dependable exclusive relationship that is unchallenged. This is the security-base needed in order to enable individuals to function well beyond the confines of marriage and home.

Jealousy cannot be 'civilised' out of existence. It is not 'a property attitude to personal relationships'.

Erich Fromm differentiates what he calls 'erotic' love from other kinds of love and maintains that 'erotic love is exclusive, but it loves in the other person all that is alive'. He continues, 'It is exclusive only in the sense that I can fuse myself fully and intensely with one person only.' This is because that in erotic love an individual loves 'from the essence of his being', and experiences the other 'in the essence of his or her being'.

As human beings, to love and be loved are parts of our capacity to deal with reality, and in marriage we are bringing all the inward dynamics of our psyche to bear on the relationship so that our identity should be made whole. It follows that the pain of jealousy springs from the awareness that emotional treachery is not only a matter of personal alienation, but a threat to the whole fabric of the reality sense and our personal values.

There is, however, a different kind of jealousy that has nothing to do with the reality referred to above. Jealous feelings can arise unbidden and unwarranted from a deep buried sense of deprivation, emptiness and littleness stemming from early experience and environmental factors. This jealousy is not related to the actualities of the marriage situation.

We all need a sense of fullness in our relationships, and ideally this is just what the husband and wife can provide for each other. When this is lacking there is danger. Self-justification accompanied by recrimination become the order of the day.

It should be clear that marriage counselling cannot be done with one partner only. The individual can be counselled, but this is counselling someone with a marriage problem, not marriage counselling. This can, in fact, increase the problems within the marriage because only one partner is gaining insights that both need. If this happens and the other partner still refuses to come for joint counselling, the client will need ongoing help to enable him/her to cope with the new, more difficult situation.

Obviously everything that can be done to bring both partners together into a counselling relationship should be done. Sometimes one counsellor sees both partners and has separate sessions with each before concentrating on a series of triangular sessions. Sometimes husband and wife may see different counsellors and then come together as a foursome for as many sessions as may be required.

The value of these 'threesomes' and 'foursomes' is obvious. If each tells the story in the presence of the other, they can correct each other and be helped to agree as to what the real situation is. Their coming together is a gain in itself as an admission that they are both responsible for their current difficulty and both desire and intend to work it out together.

Even so, there is no guarantee of success. Jack Dominian sounds a warning note:

> One of the constant dangers of marital therapy is that therapeutic changes in one person will change the delicate balance holding the partners together causing the other partner to suffer a complete breakdown. This may take place in a situation of marked competition between the spouses in which the partnership is preserved by the ability of each to demonstrate to the other their failures and in this way maintain an image of adequacy about themselves. Furthermore, the presence of these weaknesses provides a safety valve by means of which anger and resentment can be rationally directed towards one another without a sense of injustice or feelings of guilt being experienced. The subtle change of one partner in the absence of a similar change in the other, places the person with the improvement in an immediate advantage, exposing the other to the full anxieties of his own problems and inadequacies. If this proves too much, then the result is a complete breakdown.[2]

Most counsellors work hoping for a reconciliation between husband and wife, but this elegant solution is not always possible. If a breakup still occurs in spite of the counselling that has been received, the counsellor will seek to minimise the pain experienced by both partners, and continue to offer support during the fracturing experience of divorce. The anger and distress of the marriage was a relationship of some kind. With its death there is almost bound to be grief and loneliness.

What are the distress signals indicating that a marriage is in danger? There are many, of course, so that no list could be comprehensive. Dr. Paul Johnson[3], a well-known counsellor in the U.S.A. lists the following:

1. *Absent-mindedness.* This suggests that a person is pre-occupied with anxieties, regrets and perhaps fantasies. The forgetting of courtesies, errands, birthdays and anniversaries, family arrangements, is significant.

2. *Aggressive joking.* This is a more open form of attack. On a social occasion one partner might make a joke containing a hidden jibe. The company prevents the likelihood of an immediate reaction.

3. *Apathy and inertia.* These constitute the line of least resistance. They are an unconscious protest against dissatisfaction, boredom or the general loss of interest in making the marriage work. When a man's job absorbs all his energy and the

family drains the woman of all her resources, the couple cease to celebrate their joy in each other. On a B.B.C. radio programme during which marriage problems were discussed, James Hemming said: 'Everyone needs three good hugs a day.'

4. *Compulsive activity.* This can result from a persistent desire to escape from some inner anxiety, such as guilt, inferiority feelings, insecurity or a deterioration in relationships. The tendency to act in this way may not be caused by the marriage, but problems with the marriage may give it a new impetus. It can be the wife who keeps herself always busy at home and elsewhere, or the husband who increases his work-load in order not to have to spend too much time with the family.

5. *The establishing of taboos.* Here each point of disagreement between the spouses is sealed off by suppression; it becomes a taboo subject. 'This shrinks the common ground on which the couple can meet conversationally, and creates mounting tension as they hold themselves in, and keep back from dangerous precincts, lest they tread on each other's toes and provoke a quarrel.'

6. *The loss of common interests.* This may happen gradually and not be noticed in its early stages. Each can become absorbed in his or her separate interests, so that they do fewer things together, and have less enthusiasm for doing them. When courting, a man may have played tennis because that was his girl friend's consuming passion. Now they are married he may no longer feel the need to pretend to an interest that was never really his. A couple's private lives can become two separate worlds.

7. *Defensive tactics.* The foregoing can be seen as the defensive tactics they are. They raise barriers between partners and, if they lack insight and the strong desire to remedy the situation, life can become a struggle to keep on getting even with each other.

The way in which the above attitudes lead to the breakdown in communication, or the establishing of a quarrelling pattern, is not difficult to perceive. Counselling can lead to a clearer understanding of what is happening and the recognition of the need for adjustments within the marriage patterns. More than that, it can make specific the need for finding positive ways of enriching the marriage. 'Marriage enrichment' courses, which started in the U.S.A., have spread to this country. Some churches and counselling organisations are beginning to be active in this field.

An essential ingredient in such courses is learning how to express appreciation for whatever is valued in the other, and to explore each other's needs and ways of meeting them. There is also an emphasis on the importance of the 'now'. The present moment is all that we have. The resolution to ensure that 'today will be a good day' can make all the difference to a marriage and to life itself.

A further emphasis is on the fact that although parenthood is a good and important part of married life, the union should not depend upon it. After all, one half and possibly two-thirds of married life is not involved in parenthood, so the worthwhileness of the relationship must not be allowed to depend on the presence of children within the family circle.

The point needs to be made that if one partner wins an argument, there is a sense in which they both lose. Bitter arguments are akin to war — there are no real winners.

The handling of upsets is studied, the basic rule being that when it is necessary for one partner to raise a troublesome issue, he/she should always start with how he/she feels and not with the criticism. The verbal exchange should not begin with one saying to the other, 'You should not have done/said . . .' because that always puts the other on the defensive. The exchange should begin with the speaker's feelings, i.e. 'I felt really upset, or angry, when you did/said . . .' There is then a hope that the other will tune in to the partner's feelings and not feel the need for self-defence and counter-attack.

We hear so much about marriage being a matter of 'give and take'; but is fifty/fifty the ideal? Is a bargaining approach the most fruitful one to follow? 'I'll give up this interest or that friend if you will do this and that.' This kind of approach can lead to an equality of hurt, to an equation of diminishment.

We would argue that marriage need not be seen as a lifelong massive compromise. The equation need not be fifty/fifty. True equality suggests a hundred/hundred equation where each — secure in the 'one-flesh' relationship — can give freedom to the other. The ideal is a partnership of equality based on personhood. If, however, in a particular marriage relationship this seems impossible, the couple can be encouraged to move the fifty/fifty up the scale to, say, seventy-five/seventy-five, and still keep the ideal in mind.

You are mine and I am yours in love,
I am I and you are you in thought,
Independently we share our lives together.

Before leaving the marriage relationship and moving on to other matters, there is a question likely, in the future, to be brought increasingly into marriage counselling — that of artificial insemination. Husbands and wives who find it impossible to have a child will more and more have the option presented to them of AIH (artificial insemination by husband) or AID (artificial insemination by donor).

In the first case, when the wife is unable to conceive through normal sexual intercourse, the husband's sperm is inserted artificially. This is not a natural and pleasurable way of conceiving, but seeing the resulting child belongs to both parents there seems no reason why psychological or emotional problems need arise.

The second case (AID) seems to many to be a more doubtful procedure. When the inability of the wife to conceive is due to the infertility of the husband, the sperm of a 'donor' is inserted, artificially. The resulting child is the wife's but not the husband's. This is done only with the full agreement of the husband, but it is impossible for him to project himself into the future and imagine precisely how he will feel as the father of a child of his wife's, by an unknown donor. Some husbands can take this quite happily. Indeed some couples are asking for a second child from the same donor, and this can sometimes be arranged. (In Britain, medical students are often volunteer donors over a period of five years). Other husbands, however, cannot tolerate the thought or the actuality. One said, 'I couldn't bear it. I'm terribly jealous. It is just as though my wife has been unfaithful to me.' Having given permission, this is an unreasonable attitude, but feelings in such a case are not always under rational control.

Counselling couples in this delicate area is very demanding. It must be completely non-directive. It must never be possible for the counsellor to be held responsible for the decision made.

COUNSELLING THE DIVORCED

We have referred to divorce as a 'fracturing experience'. The fact that it is easier in a legal sense, does not mean that it is easy emotionally. Divorcees are often misunderstood and left alone in consequence. One-time friends do not feel at ease, and are uncertain as to how they should behave towards them. A divorce can still be, in some circles, 'much less respectable than a bereavement'. (This latter is another event that can make a difficulty for some friends to relate to the bereaved).

Divorce can also issue in difficult legal, financial and family matters which may increase the divorcee's own sense of isolation and failure. Those with strong religious beliefs relating to the indissolubility of marriage may have a great deal of guilt to work through.

Divorcees then — we are speaking generally, of course, for some find divorce a great relief after years of stress — are very often lonely and uncertain. They may feel condemned by relatives, friends and acquaintances. Feelings of self-doubt may become strong indeed. The divorce has solved a whole range of problems, but it has also created others, some of which may be unexpected.

The children of the marriage are a major source of concern. They have a relationship with both parents, and invariably one parent has the major responsibility of helping them at what could be the most difficult period of their lives. Some children have strong guilt feelings, believing they have themselves contributed to the failure of their parents' marriage.

Sometimes divorced people find their own social life restricted, and this, too, can affect the children, who may have less contact with adults as a consequence. Children are often emotionally disturbed; some will be permanently scarred.

Organisations now exist for the express purpose of helping divorcees to find the social life they need. They tend not to be invited to events at which as marrieds they were made welcome, and may feel uncertain about entertaining others, especially members of the opposite sex. Divorce also brings with it sexual deprivation that sometimes is problematical.

Counselling divorcees means giving them the opportunity to talk about their feelings, whatever these may be (i.e. guilt, anger, inadequacy, anxiety, etc.) It may also be possible to suggest ways in which they can establish new relationships, so that the future — seeming less black — can be faced with greater confidence.

FAMILY THERAPY

In family therapy the family becomes the unit with which the therapist works.

For a long time in Britain, it was the custom at Child Guidance Clinics for the mother of a troubled child to be seen, usually by a social worker, while the child was being seen by a psychiatrist. Some mothers objected to this for it suggested, even if it was not stated, that her child was probably not wholly to blame for his/her condition. Family therapy, which started in the 1950s in the U.S.A., is the natural development from child psychiatry. A leading exponent of family therapy is A.C. Robin Skynner[4] of the Tavistock Clinic, who developed his work through his interest in group psychotherapy and his work in a Child Guidance Clinic. He sees a good deal of individual psychopathology giving way to new forms by focussing on the treatment of 'natural systems', the family being one of these.

The simultaneous treatment of a whole family is a promising development. In twelve or less sessions many families acquire skills that can and do improve — and sometimes transform — the life of the whole family and every individual in it. Whatever affects one part of the family organism, affects every other part. Just as emotional disease spreads through infection, so does any infection of emotional *health*.

The goal of family therapy includes the opening up of lines of communication between all family members; the interrupting of any damaging interaction that might be operating; the increasing of awareness of their essential interdependence; the discovering of the source of both pain and pleasure in the family; the perceiving and implementing of more flexible, satisfying and responsible ways of relating.

There has developed, even in its short history, a variety of different methods of family therapy, the 'conjoint family therapy' of Virginia M. Satir[5] being among the better known. During the first session with a family, Satir describes their task in this way:

> As you know, we work with families here. And we have found that when one member has pain, all share this pain in some way. Our task is to work out ways in which everyone can get more pleasure from family life. Because I am sure that at one time this family had better times.

She points back to the time when the family life was better than it is now, and encourages hope that the present situation can be improved.

The therapist helps families to look at what they are doing to each other. He seeks to reduce their fears; to increase their self-esteem; to encourage everyone — from the youngest to the oldest member — to express their feelings. He helps each individual to see how he/she looks to others, never allows one person to speak for another, 'interprets anger as hurt', and pushes everyone in the direction of openness towards others.

We have used the word 'therapist' in the singular, but interviews with the family are usually conducted by a pair of therapists, male and female. Two pairs of eyes and ears are better than one. One of the therapists will be more active; the second more of an an observer. Interviews may be held in the family home, which has certain advantages, or the whole family may be asked to come to a clinic or centre.

One of the obvious advantages of this kind of therapy is the fact that the family members are living together between sessions, and can keep each other up to the mark. An individual client in a one-to-one relationship can let himself become slack and pretend at the next session that he has been implementing his insights all the time. Not so with family therapy. If someone reverts, the other members will notice and probably remonstrate. They can become their own therapists. And because of this, sessions are more widely spaced than is usual with one-to-one counselling.

Family therapy is necessary when one member of the family has become the patient, or client, on whom the projections of other family members have become centred. He is the family scapegoat. The others can say, 'The trouble is with him or her', when in fact it belongs to the whole family situation.

This scapegoating is as old as the family itself. As far back as 1763 a Select Committee of the House of Commons reported that some patients in the country's asylums were there as 'a way of solving family and social problems'.[6] So it has taken us a long time to wake up to the need for family therapy. It is undoubtedly a tool that will be used increasingly in the future.

Jay Hayley and Lynn Hoffman encouraged five leading family therapists to reveal their working styles, strategies and approaches. Here is an extract from the introduction to this interesting publication:

> Family therapists are distinct as a group largely because of a common assumption: if the individual is to change, the context in which he lives must change. The unit of treatment is no longer the person even if only a single person is interviewed; it is the set of relationships in which the person is embedded. Out of family therapy has come what is, perhaps, one of the major questions of this century: whether deviant and violent behaviour by individuals is adaptive to the intimate social systems in which they currently live.[7]

The fourteen years that have passed since this book appeared have confirmed the value and importance of this way of helping troubled families and the individuals who form them.

REFERENCES

1. Jack Dominian, *Marital Breakdown*, Penguin Books, 1971, p.14.
2. Jack Dominian, op. cit., 1971, p.144.
3. Paul Johnson, *Pastoral Ministration*, Nisbet, 1955, pp.121–124.
4. A.C. Robin Skynner, *One flesh: Separate persons*, Constable, 1976.
5. Virginia M. Satir, *Conjoint Family Therapy, A Guide to Theory & Technique*. Science and Behaviour Books, 1964.
6. A.D. Leigh, *The Historical Development of British Psychiatry*, Vol.1, Pergamon, 1961.
7. Jay Hayley and Lynn Hoffman, *Techniques of Family Therapy*, New York, Basic Books, 1967.

8 Two Major Enemies

Living as we do in such a complex world, and being complex ourselves, it is not surprising that human problems are diverse and manifold. There are many enemies that attack our peace of mind, that challenge our sense of the goodness — even, at times, the worthwhileness — of this life of ours.

Sometimes we feel with Robert Browning that 'all's right with the world' but, more frequently we are perplexed by all those evidences of imperfection. There is a blight that affects us all.

To try to bring our human troubles under two main headings is to lay ourselves open to the charge of over-simplification. But seeing it is impossible to examine every aspect of life, a process of selection is necessary and, we believe, desirable.

Whenever we are asked the main reasons why people seek counselling help we find ourselves talking about relationship (mainly marital and family) problems, and then moving on to those arch-enemies, anxiety and depression. These are the subject of this chapter.

ANXIETY

Since W.H. Auden called this 'The age of anxiety', the phrase has become a cliché, but it is as good and relevant a description as any. There has never been an age that has been anxiety-free. Great literature and drama has struggled with the subject throughout the centuries. The Book of Job is concerned with it; St. Augustine's writings centre around what he called man's 'restless soul'; Pascal wrote about human misery; Kierkegaard based his whole philosophy on dread; Heidegger said, 'Self-existence is worry'.

Hence all the talk about security — social security, national security, collective security. We demand security against sickness, against unemployment, against old age, and in many of these areas a measure of security is offered. But it is inadequate.

Perhaps we should challenge this craven quest for security, however understandable it is. Amelia Earhart, a young pioneer airwoman wrote to her mother (in a letter read only after she had disappeared for ever into the void): 'Even though I have lost, the adventure was worthwhile. Our family *tends to be too secure*'.

Anxiety has been called 'the dizziness of freedom'. If we were fully automated, anxiety would be unknown to us. But we sense our own freedom which makes life unpredictable. We can do this *or* that, so choices have to be made. Which shall it be? We want to make the right choice, but the consequences are often uncertain. Having made the choice, we cannot help wondering what would have happened if we had decided otherwise.

The unfree person need not be anxious. Freedom involves responsibility; responsibility involves anxiety. Anxiety is very often linked with guilt, because accountability is involved. He may not know for what or to whom he is held responsible, and yet the feeling persists.

The appeal of the totalitarian structure, the closed system — whether political or religious — lies here. These take over the ordering of the lives of their members and devotees. Obedience is all that matters. Orders and concepts must not be challenged. Here is security indeed for the fainthearted, but it is at the expense of their full humanity.

Seeing, then, that if we are to be free we are bound to know anxiety, the problem of anxiety is co-extensive with human life. The tragedy is that it so easily gets out of hand, and becomes one of the root causes of neurosis. When this happens, character development is distorted, and damaging attitudes to the self and to others mar the enjoyment of life.

There is a straightforward kind of anxiety that can be linked with the external, objective world. If we are in a hostile environment or a dangerous situation, a degree of anxiety is right and may be a good thing.

Then there is the anxiety over the control of unruly impulses in relation to others, perhaps to do with sexual desire or aggressiveness.

Anxiety may arise because of feelings of personal inadequacy, inferiority and weakness, from the lack of self-confidence generally.

It is useful and necessary to distinguish between anxiety and fear. They are linked, but the difference is their intensity. Fear is a sharply defined immediate and intense reaction to a specific object or situation. Anxiety is 'fear thinly spread', a long drawn out state of apprehensiveness. Fear has concrete, nameable objects in view: anxiety may not. It is sometimes said that fear is an emotional *problem*, while anxiety is an emotional *mystery*. It is not so much a threat as the feeling of being threatened. The dread may be faceless, in all probability it has to do with a person's inner reality.

Anxiety may take two forms, either being haunted by the sense of feeling hemmed in and trapped, or the feeling of being dangled in existence, condemned to live without any means of support. The first suggests confinement or enclosure. The second portrays openness, rootlessness, with no anchorage in life.

For the anxious person every situation, however mild in character, is experienced as a trial. He expects to be found wanting, useless, and therefore properly condemned. The behaviour of others is interpreted through these negative expectations, so that there is no objectivity in any of his personal assessments. With such a self-image he is constantly on the lookout for hitherto unrecognised deficiencies. There is also resentment at the behaviour of others which is interpreted as hurtful, critical and unsympathetic.

Any situation which fails to go according to plan, or any unprepared-for event, occasions acute distress. Even when all is reasonably well, disaster is always round the corner. Slight delay in the arrival of relative or friend denotes a fatal accident. The non-delivery of an expected letter means something catastrophic has happened.

Freud saw the trauma of birth as the prototype of all anxiety experiences, because this was the beginning of the separation of the child from the mother.

Even so, the baby continues for several months fully to identify with the mother. The realisation of separateness comes to the child gradually, but as this happens, anxiety and fear come to birth within him. When the sense of primary identification has been lost, and the infant realises he is a separate being, there follows the sense of dependence and helplessness.

From now on, the child becomes aware of danger. Mother goes away. Where to? Will she return? The child's anxiety becomes obvious to the mother. She may then ask herself what she has done wrong. The fact is simply that anxiety has become part of the child's experience, and her task now is to minimise it in so far as she can, and help him to learn to handle it.

But even during the period of primary identification, the child will have known moments — if not longer periods — of anxiety, perhaps of panic. After all, no mother is always available to meet the child's need of physical and emotional nutrition. The mother's acceptance and sustenance of the child gives him a sense of his own worth; a sense that life is good; a sense of wellbeing. That basic relationship is different for every child, and even for the individual child it will fluctuate from time to time. In some cases anxiety out-weighs the required build-up of confidence, so basic trust is never achieved.

Some authorities maintain that all the major neuroses have their origin in the first year of life, in the adequacy or otherwise of the mothering process.

Having seen that some degree of anxiety is a normal part of every life, the fact is that it can become so intense that it robs existence of all joy and meaning. Anxiety can take on a whole range of neurotic forms. Harry Guntrip published a book in the U.S.A. dealing with the subject of 'anxiety'. He reissued the identical book in Britain in which he used the term 'mental pain'. We know what we mean when referring to physical pain, but some are perplexed at the idea of mental pain. This is what we experience when anxiety goes beyond certain limits.

The following descriptions of neurotic conditions are taken from Charles Rycroft's book entitled *Anxiety and Neurosis*

Anxiety-neurosis

Patients who are said to be suffering from anxiety-neurosis complain of being anxious, tense, irritable, worried, 'on edge', 'strung-up', etc., and they are, or claim to be, persistently anxious. Their anxiety is 'free-floating', in the sense that it may, unless they are phobic, be provoked by any and every circumstance and forms a background to everything they do.[1]

Anxiety-neurosis very often occurs following a change in the person's way of life. It might be leaving school or home and moving into a work situation or tertiary education. Some people are vulnerable at every crisis point in their lives, such as marriage, parenthood, promotion (or *not* gaining promotion), right through to retirement. Change is experienced throughout life as a threat.

Obsessional neurosis

The symptoms of obsessional neurosis are of two kinds: compulsive or intrusive thoughts and images, and compulsive acts or rituals. Compulsive thoughts differ from normal thinking in that they are alien to the patient's conscious attitudes and values and are experienced by him as intruders and interrupters of his spontaneous flow of thoughts and feelings . . .

Compulsive actions are usually in themselves trivial and derive their distressing quality from the fact that the patient nonetheless feels compelled to repeat them and becomes anxious if he fails to do so. They can conveniently be thought of as privately constructed superstitious rituals. Clothes, the objects on a mantelpiece or table, have to be laid out in a particular, usually symmetrical manner. Washing has to be done according to a particular routine and certain objects must either be avoided or touched whenever passed.[2]

Charles Rycroft makes an interesting contrast between an obsessional neurosis and a phobia. Although neither the phobic nor the obsessional really knows what provokes his fear or anxiety, the phobic imagines he does and so tries to avoid it, whereas the obsessional does not know but seeks to control it by his repetitive ritual.

Hysteria

The nearest to a precise definition of hysteria that one is likely to reach is that it is a condition in which (a) the patient complains of physical symptoms which are nonetheless unaccompanied by any signs of organic disease, (b) the symptoms correspond to the patient's idea of how his body works and not to the actual facts of anatomy and physiology and (c) the patient is not anxious, resists the idea that his symptoms may be of psychological origin and reacts evasively to all attempts to discover whether he has psychological and personal problems.[3]

The hysteric 'converts' an emotional problem into a physical symptom such as paralysis, blindness, loss of voice, fits and fainting attacks etc. This 'conversion' is an unconscious process, but there is always an end to be achieved.

The use of tranquilising drugs in order to help the over-anxious person is now so widespread and prolific that many medical authorities are issuing warnings that should be heeded. Dr. C.A.H. Watts writes:

Soon after the antidepressant drugs were introduced a number of new tranquillisers were produced and these were said to have the same effect on anxiety as the antidepressive group had on depression. They certainly relieved the tension in anxiety and were less dangerous than the quick acting barbiturates, but still, if taken for any length of time, the patient finds it very hard to do without them. The majority of patients who find comfort in their tranquillisers are reluctant to stop taking them even when the crisis which caused the anxiety has passed.[4]

How, then, can counselling help the anxiety-prone person? The degree of need varies with every client. Those who were not so seriously disturbed in their childhood relationships, will not need such 'depth' treatment as those whose early experience has been fraught in anxiety-provoking ways. In every case it will be the counselling relationship itself that offers the greatest hope of healing.

Those not so seriously damaged may respond quite quickly to the genuine interest and concern shown to them. Others delay their own healing by the inner conflict that prevents them from co-operating in the help being offered. They may feel ashamed at having to seek help, so there may be some resistance that must first be overcome.

The anxious person is bound, initially, to become dependent on the counsellor. This, too, may be resented by the client, and encouragement might be needed by the counsellor. He can assure the client that the great majority have stronger dependent needs arising out of inner anxiety and insecurity, than they admit. In any case, although over-dependence will need to be worked through, dependence itself is not to be derided. Those who cannot depend at all cannot love.

The transference process is bound to come into operation. The client may expect at first to be treated by the counsellor in the same way as he was treated by his parents, because this is what has been built into him. He must learn to be free enough within himself to react *differently* towards the counsellor from the way he habitually reacted towards his parents. He can say what he genuinely thinks and feels.

There must be an emotional rapport. If the anxiety state has as its basic cause a deficiency in the love relation, then healing will not come simply from a scientific analysis. The feeling level must be reached. The client's ego will be strengthened to the extent that the counsellor becomes a mature parent figure, who can encourage the necessary growth towards maturity in the client. It is this human caring that makes the anxiety more bearable and, eventually, whatever 'cure' there is will be the result of the 'care' offered by the counsellor and responded to by the client.

These brief comments must not be taken to mean that every anxious person can be guaranteed complete healing. All emotional healing takes time, and it is rarely complete. But most clients can be helped towards a greater understanding, a more effective control, and a more responsible functioning.

EXISTENTIAL ANXIETY

There is an experience of anxiety even greater than those already mentioned. It is anxiety about existence itself — not existence in general, but one's own existence. Anxiety at this level can lead to complete despair and then on to the severest depression. This chapter is entitled 'Two major enemies'. Existential anxiety is the link between the two.

There are three kinds of crises in life. The first are called 'developmental' and are 'natural'. Stages of life such as infancy, adolescence, middle-age, come into this category. The second are 'accidental' in the sense that they *need* not happen, or happen rarely. These include sickness, marriage (!), and bereavement. The third kind is not a whole range of events and situations. It is the emotional/intellectual crisis when we ask fundamental questions about existence, especially our own. Has it any meaning, purpose, value? If so, what? This is an anxiety generated by the awareness of our own finitude.

There is a famous legend on inescapable death:

A servant ran to his master in fright, saying he had been jostled and threatened by Death in the market-place of Baghdad and wished therefore to go as

rapidly as possible to Samarra where Death would not find him. His master
let him go and then went himself to the market place and seeing Death there
asked him why he had threatened his servant. To this Death replied that it
was not a threat but a gesture of surprise that he should see in Baghdad the
man with whom he had an appointment that night in Samarra.

Most people try to forget the only certainty in life, which is death, but the
reality is always there. The feeling that our very being is under threat is never
far away. There are accidents, diseases, bereavements. There is loneliness,
insecurity, weakness, fear. It is often asserted that sometimes what looks like a
religious problem hides an emotional problem, and this we would not deny. The
contrary is also very often true. What seems like a purely emotional problem
may conceal a fundamental religious issue in which deep down the individual
is concerned about ultimate questions. A 'value vacuum' is part of today's reality,
and it is often our novelists and playwrights who underline this for us. For
instance, what is the message of Samuel Beckett's *Waiting for Godot*, in which
the characters are looking and longing for a meaning that has eluded them and
still eludes them at the end?

The knowledge that he will die is the background music that plays faintly in
the distance throughout the whole of life, even when we try to ensure that we
do not hear it. A desperate concern about existence itself is the shadow that
touches all other anxieties and gives them power over us.

The counsellor needs the courage to allow the client to articulate these
fundamental questions. He may even need to encourage him to do so, because
to leave them unasked may be damaging indeed. Everyone needs to bring out
into the open such questions as: What does life mean? Why are we here? What
is our individual relation to existence as a whole? A hospital patient said, 'As
long as nobody asks the big questions, you can ignore them and let them be, but
when they are asked you cannot put them down again until you have the
answer.' The counselling room may be for the client the only place where he
can face his own anxiety and seek ways of incorporating it into his self-awareness.
What a client brings in the first place is something urgent, an immediate pressure
and concern. But at another level there may be something more important still
— the existential anxiety of which he may be only dimly aware.

It is natural for the client to fear getting into touch with his deep despair, but
this may be necessary. Many of our contemporaries are teetering on the brink
of suicide, sometimes for no obvious reasons. They feel inwardly devastated. A
client writes between sessions:

The cries for help come from my heart. My head is empty. I can't think
properly. The world doesn't seem real any more. . . . Whatever is inside me
is bent on destruction. I must be destroyed because I am evil.
I'm forcing myself to write this letter because I had this sudden desire to feel
pain. Perhaps you might call it a wild imagination but before picking up this
pen, I wanted to use a knife on myself, to let the blood flow freely . . .
If you just send me an empty envelope it would be enough to keep me going
till we meet again.

Counsellors discover that this depth of despair is more common than most people imagine. It raises issues that will need to be looked at in the final chapter. What does, what can the counsellor do in such a dire situation? He holds on to the conviction that emotional pain can be seen as a harbinger of hope. The contemporary Russian poet Yevgeny Yevtushenko concludes a remarkable poem in this way:

> But people insist, and I
>   can't cope with it,
> That I'm no good,
>   have so few ties with life.
>
> But if I connect with so
>   many things,
> I must stand for something,
>   apparently, have some value?
> And if I stand for nothing
>   why then
>   do I suffer and weep?[5]

Why indeed? Our suffering and weeping must have a meaning beyond itself. Our tenderness, our misgivings, our sensitivity, say something about life itself, for it is the dead nerve that feels no pain.

Henry Miller, the American writer, concludes the second volume of his autobiographical novel in this way:

Once I thought that I had been wounded as no man ever had. Because I felt thus I vowed to write this book. But long before I began the book the wound had healed. Since I had sworn to fulfil my task I re-opened the horrible wound. Let me put it another way ... Perhaps in opening the wound, my own wound, I closed other wounds, other people's wounds. Something dies, something blossoms. To suffer in ignorance is horrible. To suffer deliberately, in order to understand the nature of suffering and abolish it for ever, is quite another matter. The Buddha had one fixed thought in mind all his life, as we know. It was to eliminate human suffering. Suffering is unnecessary, But one has to suffer before he is able to realise that this is so. It is only then, moreover, that the true significance of human suffering becomes clear. At the last desperate moment — when one can suffer no more! — something happens which is in the nature of a miracle. The great open wound which was draining the blood of life closes up, the organism blossoms like a rose. One is 'free' at last. . . .[6]

It was Miller's conviction that there is healing for life's wounds, that there is a point beyond which pain is not allowed. Which ties up with Kierkegaard's conviction that if a man is destroyed by despair it must be because he has not experienced it deeply enough. To touch bottom is to discover an indestructible reality. In the final analysis, good is more comprehensive than evil.

DEPRESSION

To feel depressed is a perfectly normal experience. Everyone has fluctuations of mood, and feels a 'bit down' at times. This is part of life, and not what this section is about.

Let us begin with a description of the kind of depression we are concerned with here. Gerald Priestland is the B.B.C.'s religious correspondent, and following the death, by suicide, of Jacky Gillott, he broadcast a talk (on October 4th, 1980) containing this extract:

> ... depression is like a dark mist lurking in the corners of the room, always there, always ready to come surging forward and rising up to envelop you. It is blackness, it is emptiness, it is meaninglessness and total inner despair. Others may think you are fortunate, but *you* know it is all an empty fraud, and that one day the hollow balloon will burst, you will be found out and your crime exposed. What crime? You don't know; you only know you are guilty; and you can hear them coming down the corridor to get you. The penalty, of course, is death and you might as well be your own executioner.

Priestland was describing *his own experience* in an attempt to explain Jacky Gillott's death. They had worked together on the same programme ('neither of us recognised the depression of the other'), which shows how we hide ourselves from one another. Priestland has survived and thanks God for modern drugs and psychiatry.

Here are a few further partial descriptions:

> You cease entirely to care about your family and friends. No one can get through to you. You hate them for trying and hate them for not trying. You hate people for caring because you feel unlovable and you hate them for not caring because you want to be loved. Either way you lose. The conflicts that opposing feelings like these bring are unbearable.
>
> The sight of other people being happy or efficient or busy makes you realise how useless you are and how helpless the situation you are in. Enormous feelings of resentment arise at having to meet other people's perfectly reasonable needs.
>
> Any religious faith you had just vanishes and what takes its place is not just absence — which might possibly be bearable — but a frightening sense of despair, a kind of angry despair which is very self-destructive.
>
> I lack the courage to die and I lack the courage to live.
>
> You get into a state where you don't care about anyone ... You see life as a big black hole which is gradually swallowing you up. At first you feel sorry for yourself and then you even stop feeling sorry for yourself. You wonder what you have done. Why is it happening to you? You don't know what you have done. All you know is that the whirlpool you are in scares you stiff and you want to get out but don't know how.[7]

It is usual to differentiate between 'reactive' depression and 'endogenous' depression. (The foregoing descriptions belong to the latter category.)

'Reactive' depression is perfectly understandable. Something distressing happens and the individual 'reacts' by becoming depressed. It might be a broken love affair, the loss of a job, the betrayal by a friend, the death of a loved one. The spirit falls and a depression sets in. How could it be otherwise?

'Endogenous' depression is of a different order. It comes from within. It cannot be accounted for by external circumstances. It may last for several weeks, even months — a mystery to all concerned. Dr. C.A.H. Watts writes:

> Patients suffering from endogenous depression are often very perplexed by what has happened to them. 'I have no pains, I have no worry, but I feel awful, I just cannot understand myself', is one way of expressing their feelings. One woman told her doctor, 'There is nothing wrong with my organs, it is just what holds me together which is missing'.[8]

Sufferers from endogenous depression should always be encouraged to seek medical help.

Physical characteristics of this kind of depression include: insomnia, marked by early morning waking; loss of appetite, energy and sex-drive; aches and pains. Psychological characteristics include: continuous low mood, but at its worst in the morning; a general slowing down in mental activity; agitation, although this may vary; feelings of inferiority, hopelessness and guilt; hallucinations may occur.

As with anxiety, the origin of depression lies away back in infancy. It seems that any breach in the mother/child relationship in the first two to three years — but particularly if this should happen in the first nine months — can have a lasting effect. How does an infant handle the ambivalence of both loving and hating the same source-person? Harry Guntrip writes:

> The pathological guilt felt over hating someone who is also loved, turns the hate into self-hate, until all the patient's energy seems to become absorbed in self-torture, and the personality sinks into a paralysed state so far as external activity goes. There is, however, plenty of energy available for the attack on the self. In extreme cases the only activity that seems to be left to the patient is a secret intense self-accusation and self-punishment, in a personality which is more or less immobilised and out of touch in relation to the external world. One of the far-reaching insights with which Freud penetrated the hidden secrets of this seriously disturbed mental condition, was his observation that the patient (i.e. originally the child), not being able to tolerate hating his external love-object in reality, mentally 'internalised' him. That is to say he took the bad side of his love-object, as it were, into himself, and identified himself with it. He could then hate the bad parent inside himself, which was at the same time self-hate or turning of his hate inwards, and love the good parent in his outer world.[9]

Depression, then, in its origins is linked with aggression. The child, feeling angry and fearing to admit to hostile feelings towards the mother, turns them inwards and hurts himself. The damage done is long-term. Every child has some experience of what is now being called 'primal pain'. He survives by repressing most of this, it is forcibly *not remembered*. This defence mechanism makes great demands upon an individual's psychic energy. He is using it to *de*press strong forces, and therefore has little strength left to function. Some depressives just cannot get out of bed in the morning, and this is not malingering. They simply have no energy to spare for the normal business of living. Even when they find sufficient strength to seek counselling help, the sense of depletion has to be reckoned with, especially at the start. Their ability to respond, to co-operate, to begin to take initiatives is strictly limited.

Which leads to the question of what can be done for people suffering from a depressive illness?

They should be encouraged, and perhaps helped to find the best kind of medical help. Electro-convulsive therapy is very effective in some cases, even though how this happens is by no means fully understood. Anti-depressant drugs can enable many to function well enough so as to benefit from counselling and psychotherapy.

One of the aims of counselling is to help the client towards a new perspective on his suffering. In the early stages it will be clear that whatever healing may come is some distance away, so a new method of handling the present experience is desirable. One such way is suggested by J. Neville Ward:

> Wisdom would seem to be not a facility for excluding anxiety, resentment and regret, because that could mean denying facts, disowning part of oneself. Wisdom is a matter of letting the black thought come yet keeping a margin all round it in the mind, so that it is seen in relation to other thoughts, other facts of life, which make it less formidable.[10]

Counselling involves getting alongside the client, and together finding out what is really happening both at the level of reality and of fantasy, and finding a way ahead. It also means giving the client an opportunity to ventilate his resentments at the same time helping him to see the futility of reproaching either people or circumstances. It means helping him to discover those defects in his personality growth which are making him ineffective in the present. This involves a great deal of probing into the past. The trouble is that he cannot recall the babyhood experience of destructive anger which may be the first stage in the formation of his depressive personality. But what he is likely to know is whether his family background was one in which a healthy acceptance of negative emotions was possible, and it is along that line that important facts can be teased out.

Inevitably the child fails to see the meaning of his experience, but this happens throughout life when sometimes there is no excuse. Counselling can be a process whereby we find lost meanings. T.S. Eliot wrote:

> We had the experience but missed the meaning,
> An approach to the meaning restores the experience
> In a different form, beyond any meaning
> We can assign to happiness.[11]

This kind of shared enquiry has been called the provision of 'corrective emotional experience'. It is concerned with his inner conflicts that produce guilt and aggression, and the quest for a new understanding of how childhood experience is being reactivated in the present. What happened 'there and then' can help him understand and deal with what is happening 'here and now'.

The counselling relationship should provide conditions satisfactory to the discovery and re-experiencing of the hurts of childhood in a way that will be bearable, therapeutic, and creative of hope for the future.

Depression is normally the strongest element in most suicide attempts, successful or otherwise. There is very often a combination of other factors, such as recent severe loss, lack of family or friends, bankruptcy, alcoholism, mental illness, etc. Fewer men than women attempt suicide; when they do, however, they are more likely to succeed.

Every suicide threat should be taken seriously. It is true that some play around with the thought without any serious intention, but the idea that those who threaten do not do it, is a common misconception. Suicide can and does happen without warning, but in the majority of cases, those surrounding the suicide are usually aware of the possibility. It is estimated that eight out of every ten give some specific warning.

When an individual is in the depths of despair he usually lacks sufficient ego-strength to kill himself. Because of this, improvement after the crisis should be viewed with suspicion because, when getting through the crisis, his ego-strength may rise so that he finds himself able to act. So the suicidal person is most at risk when on the way down and on the way up. He may, in fact, become more cheerful because he has decided to kill himself.

For several weeks 18 year old Muriel had been unable to attend for her weekly counselling session. The depression was so overwhelming she simply could not get out of bed. Then came relief. The depression lifted and she was well enough to come. She looked and spoke as though she was through the worst. We felt relieved for her. She actually smiled as she left the centre.

It was *that* weekend Muriel took an overdose. This was no 'cry for help', but a serious attempt to end it all. Fortunately it failed — and we can say it was fortunate because seven years later Muriel is leading a full and happy life.

We have seen that depression represents angry feelings reflected back on to the self, so suicide is the logical ultimate. A recent study of murder followed by suicide dealt with the relation between depression and aggression. The fact emerged that of every three murders committed in Britain, one is followed by the suicide of the murderer. This seems a clear demonstration of the truth of Freud's hypothesis that aggression against others and against the self are related, and to some extent interchangeable.

The counsellor's task is to generate hope. The feelings of the person must be taken seriously. There is no place for minimising or ridiculing them. They are the reality that is blinding him to the possibilities and alternatives that exist. Initially he may have to live on the counsellor's hope until it becomes his own.

REFERENCES

1. Charles Rycroft, *Anxiety and Neurosis*, Penguin Books, 1970, p.111.
2. Charles Rycroft, op cit. pp.116, 117, 118.
3. Charles Rycroft, op. cit. p.120.

4. C.A.H. Watts, *Depression — the Blue Plague*, Priory Press Ltd, 1973, p.43.
5. *The Poetry of Yevgeny Yevtushenko*, Selected, edited and translated by George Reavey, Calder & Boyars, Ltd., 1966, p.47.
6. Henry Miller, *Plexus: The Rosy Crucifixion*, a Panther Book, 1969, p.460.
7. Jack Dominian, *Depression*, Fontana, 1976, pp.18, 19, 20.
8. C.A.H. Watts, op. cit. p.11.
9. Harry Guntrip, *Healing the Sick Mind*, Allen & Unwin, 1964, p.46.
10. J. Neville Ward, *Friday Afternoon*, Epworth Press, 1976.
11. T.S. Eliot, *Four Quartettes. The Complete Poems & Plays*, Faber & Faber, 1969, p.186.

9   The Human Life Cycle

A feeling of uniqueness can be exhilarating or demoralising according to the ego-state of the person concerned. There are those who cannot tolerate feeling different from their neighbours or peers, let alone from the rest of the world. This sense of alienation and isolation brings many to the point of despair.

Yet, despite feelings to the contrary, we all do have much in common, in that we share a number of basic, external, environmental experiences of life. Each of us spent up to nine months in the womb, and survived the intense experience of birth. We all received attention, of whatever quality, from at least one available adult, otherwise we could not have sustained existence for many hours.

In one way or another we each survived the hazards of childhood's early years. The majority of us faced the crisis of going to school, and have faced, or will face, adolescence, growing up, middle-age, and old age. Without exception we will all die.

The intention in the following study is to indicate the importance of the counsellor having a working knowledge of the significant developmental stages in the life cycle, so that he may understand his client. Reverting, under stress, to the behaviour pattern of an earlier, less complex stage of development, is fairly common practice, and needs to be recognised for what it is.

It has been acknowledged throughout the ages that life is not a static, plateau experience. The sphynx asked a riddle which suggested three stages in the life of man. Confucious referred to five stages, each of about ten years. Shakespeare's seven stages are, perhaps, more familiar. Erikson[1] added one more, making eight, and we hope to show that a ninth is deserving of recognition and consideration.

1   THE PRE-NATAL PERIOD

The stage not included by the others mentioned is the pre-natal. Let us, therefore, start before the beginning, so to speak, for, in a sense, this is surely the most crucial phase of man's development.

In the nine months prior to birth he lives in the moist, even warmth of his mother's womb. In this protected environment he re-enacts the whole evolutionary process, starting as a minute speck of protoplasm, changing into a kind of fish with vestigial gills, and then into something resembling a reptile, before developing into a monkey-like creature which presages his ultimate form.

Perhaps 're-enacts' is too positive a word because, in fact, this process is not something he initiates or can control, but something that happens to him simply because his parents are members of the human species, and he must repeat the pattern.

At this stage he is wholly parasitic, living totally upon his mother. He and his mother are physically one consequently, it seems, whatever happens to her affects him. A Pavlovian-type experiment carried out on a number of women in late pregnancy, illustrates this kind of 'rapport'. Each woman was given a minute electric shock simultaneously with the ringing of a bell. To this stimulus she and the foetus reacted by 'jumping'. This was repeated many times. Eventually only the bell was rung without the shock, and the foetus still reacted as previously. After birth these babies were subjected at intervals to the same sort of bell-ringing and, for a brief period, they continued to respond as in the womb.

It has been common knowledge for a long time that if a pregnant woman contracts German Measles at a certain stage of the development of the foetus, then he is likely to be born malformed, blind or deaf.

D.H. Stott, in his chapter 'The Child's Hazards in Utero' contained in *Modern Perspectives in International Psychiatry*, says:

> It would have been gratifying . . . to quote a large number of definitive studies. Only those relating to rubella and thalidomide can be regarded as 'proved' in the usual sense of the word. Such work as has been done has served to destroy the myth that the foetus is completely protected from outside influences. Indeed the evidence suggests that the foetus is peculiarly sensitive to its environment within the maternal host, and to stresses which affect the mother. At least the possibility has been established that the major determinants of viability, physical growth and health, mental ability and personality, may be those which operate during gestation.[2]

If the mother is addicted to drugs the infant may be born similarly addicted and even exhibit withdrawal symptons. If she smokes heavily or drinks to any extent, he will be affected. What interests us especially is the psychological repercussions from the physical condition, and these may be manifold.

The influence of genes is decisive and permanent, for physical appearance and general abilities affect every aspect of life, and although environment and culture contribute to physical development, the genes with which he was endowed at the moment of conception set a potential which, so far as physique is concerned, cannot be exceeded, however assiduous his efforts.

With personality one may be less dogmatic, but it seems to us that the embryonic personality bestowed on him in his genes, partly determines how he is treated from his earliest days. This is why controversy surrounding the heredity versus environment question has faded out of existence for most psychologists.

There are still considerable differences of opinion with regard to consciousness during the pre-natal period, but routine observation in ante and post-natal clinics indicate that extreme emotional stress in the mother often seems to coincide with hyperactivity of the foetus, and after birth it has been noted that this infant cries excessively and often has sleeping and feeding difficulties. Unequivocal conclusions a propos the infant's psychology cannot be reached on such evidence alone, but possible cause and effect deserve to be considered and kept in mind as a real possibility.

The actual birth process is thought by some authorities to account for what seems a basic anxiety in man. Bright lights, noise, bustle, loud voices, rough handling, after the dark warmth and relative quiet of the womb must, inevitably, be traumatic. Growing awareness of this fact will, it is hoped, result in more subdued labour wards, providing a gentler reception for new members of our society.

In recent years the advent of primal therapy associated, mainly, with Arthur Janov[3] involves the re-living of early experience of primal pain, including even the trauma of birth itself.

Kathleen, a forty year old, intelligent, poorly educated working woman, was frightened by the violence of her feelings and, also, by the claustrophobia which turned her day-to-day living into an exhausting struggle. She was the only child of an older mother whose labour period was difficult and extended. During therapy Kathleen latched on to the idea of the birth-trauma being a possible pre-disposing factor to much crippling anxiety and pain. An outlining of Janov's primal-therapy theory captivated her, and seemed to her to offer hope. So she pressed her therapist to let her try it.

After weeks of preparatory discussion and exploration, Kathleen felt ready for the ordeal. She lay on the floor of the therapy room surrounded by cushions (representing the womb) which were held very firmly against her. Gently she was urged to make her way out. For quite a while she struggled in vain (and by this time she was really 'in' the experience, and oblivious of the actual setting), then as pressure was gradually and spasmodically released, she emerged with groans and cries.

For some time she lay there panting and calling, 'Is anybody there? Oh, why isn't somebody there?' (It seems possible that the mother's life having been in immediate and unexpected danger, Kathleen had been temporarily neglected).

In great distress she continued to moan, re-experiencing, it seemed, the desperate sense of abandonment and isolation.

Rounding off and integrating the experience (which included asking and answering questions of the fantasised mother), took time, after which Kathleen went on her way subdued and weary.

The upshot of this one experience was immediate release from the claustrophobia which had so bedevilled her.

2 BABYHOOD

0–1½ years   Shakespeare: 'At first the infant
                            Mewling and puking in the nurse's arms'[4]
              Freud: Oral Period.
              Erikson: Trust versus mistrust.

Having survived the hazards and discomforts of birth, the new person begins the lifelong process of relating to his enviroment — sometimes with apparent pleasure, at other times with obvious pain. The majority of new babies sleep most of the time perhaps in order to protect themselves from the rigours of conscious living in the robust and alien world into which they have been hustled.

His life-script has been partly written for him but from these earliest days the child begins to learn to trust, or not to trust. He cannot do anything for himself, and depends totally on others to keep him warm and fed, simply that he might survive. Without at least a modicum of goodwill he will not continue to live. But if his basic needs are consistently met, the foundation to a life of social trust is firmly laid. Erikson sees promise of this social trust, and indeed a demonstration of it, in the manner of a baby's feeding, the depth of his sleep, and the relaxation of his bowels.

Beyond the essentials for physical survival is the need for that which will nourish the emotional life of the baby. For instance, holding and cuddling seem to be vital to his welfare. The child who is handled warmly and lovingly in this way is more responsive and 'alive', and rapport between mother and child is quickly established. Where this is absent, the body may thrive, but the 'self' will be under-nourished. If he is very fortunate the deficiency may be made good in later life, but for most the effects are always felt and manifested.

Anna typifies this kind of early deprivation. She was the only child of affluent parents and lived with them in the heart of the country in a beautiful house and home. Her every material need was met lavishly, and even fleeting whims were gratified. But her mother had not really wanted a child — she had no maternal urge — and though she gave the required physical attention to Anna, there was no warmth — no cuddling and loving.

So nothing they gave or did for her was enough — ever. She always *felt* deprived. She spent her life trying to find assurance that she was lovable, and acceptable. She *felt* unlovable. Every so often she developed unsightly rashes, symbolising her unacceptableness — her untouchableness.

When, in teenage years, she was hugged by a male relative at a family get-together, she hit him, much to the man's bewilderment and embarrassment. 'Dates' with boys ended abruptly as soon as any physical contact was made. Her infant life-script had clearly indicated to her that she was unlovable and untouchable. In her mid-twenties she was still living by it angrily, and pathetically, and in the process making life miserable for all around her.

With part of her she longed to tear up this script — to see it as fiction to be read and discarded — and to write her own; but with the other part she saw it as a valid blue-print to which she was irrevocably committed.

Not all mothers are naturally demonstrative, but it is the quality of the maternal relationship which helps to establish belief in self and others. Anna never felt a 'belonging' part of a family unit, so her life and behaviour were isolated entities without meaning, because unrelated to anything outside herself, and from this, it would seem likely, her neurosis stemmed.

Freud may have been over-stating his case when he claimed that *all* adult neuroses have their roots in the earliest years, but experience certainly seems to point there, in the majority of cases. What seems to happen is that a pattern of stimulation in some way disorganises and disturbs the infant. This pattern is repeated again and again in the parents' or family's mode of relating to him, so that the constant reinforcement makes it almost impossible for any kind of emotional reorganisation. This means that adulthood is reached with areas of inexplicable emotional discomfort.

This pre-verbal stage is, then, of enormous importance. More observable progess is made here than at any other stage. The infant learns to walk and use his hands in a purposeful way. He begins to differentiate between one person and another, and to recognise that things and people do not cease to exist when they are no longer within his range of vision. When at this stage he can allow mother out of his sight without undue anxiety or rage, then he is indicating that he has already developed some degree of trust in himself, and also in the consistency of her behaviour.

Infants vary considerably in speech development, but it usually begins during this stage and marks the start of the transition from infancy to childhood.

3   EARLY CHILDHOOD

2–5 years   Freud: Anal and genital period
Erikson: Autonomy versus shame and doubt.
Initiative versus guilt.

This stage is full of interest to the child, parents and all closely associated with him. He becomes increasingly skilled in movement, and is a bundle of dynamic energy. Every walk for a two year old is a voyage of discovery and adventure. Each flight of steps, narrow ledge, muddy puddle, pile of leaves, suggests climbing, balancing, jumping and probing activities. When hopping and skipping and dancing have become part of his repertoire, then this increase in skill fosters self-confidence which encourages emotional development.

The over-careful, nervous mother who is constantly telling her child to 'be careful, or you'll fall', 'you'll hurt yourself', is not providing the right kind of environment for the development of muscular and emotional control. There is always real danger from which a child must be protected, but by minor falls and knocks he learns to protect himself.

He now has a greater sense of physical autonomy and this is reflected in his conception of himself. For instance, from referring to himself by his name — 'John wants a biscuit' — during the early part of this period of development, he will generally move on to using the personal pronoun 'I' — 'I want a biscuit'. This marks the beginning of real independence and indicates a growing sense of personhood.

Geoffrey, a fifty year old client, brought up by a series of 'nannies', with the gardener and chauffeur for intermittent company, described how as a child up to the age of six or seven, he could never bring himself to say 'I'. The nearest he could get was to use the plural 'we' and 'us'. When out for a drive the chauffeur sometimes told him a story, and this delighted Geoffrey. On the occasions when the chauffeur was silent, he longed to ask for another story, but could not say 'Tell *me* a story'. He had to wait until 'nanny' was with him, when he could make the request quite easily, 'Tell *us* a story'. At fifty he was still unsure of himself as a person.

If a child at this stage is observed and listened to as he wanders or rushes around, it will be noted that for a lot of the time he is actually talking. In this way he is trying to build up meaningful and coherent representations of the multiplicity of impressions that are constantly impinging on him. When he makes a direct observation in the presence of an adult, he *needs* a response to confirm to himself that he is on the right lines, and that things are what they seem. What sounds absurd to the adult is wholly sensible, logical and vital to the developing child.

It has been noted that many children during the early part of this stage find the television set, radio, or telephone worrying pieces of equipment. This is not surprising. It is distinctly threatening to think of people living inside these boxes. After all, they may emerge at any time of day or night, and who is to say they are friendly?

When, as often happens, such fears have been expressed and have repeatedly evoked the response of laughter or ridicule, seeds are sown for future timidity, excessive sensitivity to criticism, and unwillingness or inability to express opinions for fear of being made to feel silly or ridiculous.

Erikson sees the major task of this stage as learning when to let go and when to hold on. This is important because it represents the child's first efforts to free himself from parental and general dominance. The acquired motor skills and muscle co-ordination have begun the process. The muscle controlling bowel action has special significance in this connection, for here there is a natural pressure from within to let go. There is also a different kind of pressure from without — particularly from the mother or nurse — as to the place and time for doing this.

At this time he makes a momentous discovery — for the first time in his life he can be in control. Hitherto mother and other adults have had complete power over him, but now there is a dramatic shift. He has a choice. He finds he can hold on — say 'no' — or let go — say 'yes'. He now recognises what is him and what is his. Revolutionary stuff, this! To some limited extent he can now control his own body, and even exert power over others. This is a crucial discovery, and it is at this stage that certain basic attitudes are established. How successfully he negotiates this take-over bid will partly determine his bias towards co-operativeness or rebelliousness in later life, and to what extent he will value or repress his own self-expression. Whether he will be able to give of himself happily and confidently, or withhold himself nervously or stubbornly, are tendencies that are 'pencilled in' at this time.

If his first efforts at self-control are successful and applauded, he experiences his first good, proud feeling about himself. If they are unsuccessful, or disapproved of he may very well grow up lacking in confidence in himself and his achievements. Maybe, too, with a vague feeling of shame.

It is not surprising that this anal stage, as it is called, is so crucial. The drama that surrounds a child's first successful bid for power must be exhilarating, albeit somewhat frightening. Life can never be quite the same again.

When Gwen sought help with her multiple problems, although articulate and able to express with relative ease what she felt, she would always hold back, inappropriately, essential pieces of her story. This would continue for a long time before she finally 'let go'. Not because there was any kind of shame or embarrassment involved in the information she held, but because of what seemed a built-in reluctance to *give* in reponse to the wishes of an outside agency. She would 'let go' when *she* chose, and the 'delivery' was frequently accompanied by a triumphant grin.

The connection between Gwen in her thirties and Gwen in her second and third year was plain to see. There was the urge to be in control of every situation; the pleasure experienced when she had the upper hand; and the panic and terror that assailed her when not in control. Air-travel and thunder-storms reduced Gwen to a quivering mass. Not being in control of the situation, *she* was out of control.

The acquisition of speech is perhaps the achievement of most practical importance during this stage, for without language, communication is limited and the child severely handicapped. Children develop at different rates; more rapidly than the norm in some areas, and less so in others. In an effort to reassure anxious mothers of late speech-developers, the illustration of Einstein and Samuel Johnson is frequently used. It seems they were well below the average rate of development in the talking area, and see what happened to them! All the same, although premature anxiety is unwarranted, the Einstein and Johnson story should not prevent parents from seeking advice if their own Albert of Samuel are remaining silent much beyond the age of two. Delayed speech *can* be due to physiological factors such as deafness, or some brain defect. It can also be a symptom of autism, and in all such cases early diagnosis is essential.

The child at this stage receives considerable satisfaction from his increasing skill in using his body as he wants, in manipulating toys which had previously frustrated him, in being able to help parents with simple tasks. Finding that he can himself 'look after' smaller children, and care for small animals, gives him pleasure and confidence.

The latter part of this two to five year old stage is designated by Freud and his followers as the genital stage. The child is aware of his sexual feelings without knowing what they are. During this period he is brought face to face with the three-sided situation of himself, his mother and his father — the oedipal situation. Considerable anxiety surrounds this phase and a great deal depends on how he is helped to handle his feelings about it.

The oedipal situation derives its name from a Greek myth which goes like this:

Oedipus was the son of Laius, King of Thebes. It was prophesied that the boy would grow up to kill his father, whereupon, to avert the tragedy, he was given by his father to a shepherd with instructions that he was to leave the boy on the mountain to die. Instead, the shepherd gave the boy to the king of another realm, where he grew to manhood. Eventually Oedipus met his real father and, being unaware of his identity, slew him in battle.

One day he returned to the land of his birth and, in return for solving a riddle, was given the queen, his mother, to wife. Still unaware of the identity of his real parents, he lived with his mother for a time as man and wife. When he finally learned the truth, in his guilt he put out his own eyes, and his mother hanged herself. Later he was destroyed by avenging deities.

Incest, with its associated guilt and tragedy, has kept the name of Oedipus, and it is applied to this stage of development where the emotions surrounding the mother/child/father interaction are very powerful.

At this time the child begins to develop a superego, which is the process of internalising his parents' attitudes and standards. This superego is generally much harsher, more domineering and tyrannical than his real parents have ever been. So now he often becomes over-controlled, repressing feelings of hatred and guilt. The oedipal period is at its most potent.

This is the time when the boy who has wanted to kill father and possess mother, and the girl who has a need to be absorbed in mother, now begin to translate these desires and needs into symbolic necessities, which continue right through adolescence. Rivalry between father and son, mother and daughter, will ebb and flow until eventually the son becomes convinced that mother is already 'booked', and that he will have to look elsewhere, outside the home, for a girl-friend of his own age. The girl, too, will have rivalry problems until she registers a similar message.

A satisfactory resolution of the oedipal crisis, then, is a further major task of this stage. In time of war when fathers were away and children brought up by mother and/or grandmother, much identity and sexual confusion often resulted which repercussed throughout life. The counselling-room is a refuge for many such who may there find for themselves insight and understanding of their feelings, and discover a way of handling them. Others battle on alone.

Drs. Blank and Lewes have said:

> One of the most disheartening phenomena is the failure of the parents to resolve their own needs for dependence and autonomy, thus causing a similar failure of resolution in their children. The cycle of neurotic and self-destructive behaviour is thus repeated from generation to generation. We are strongly convinced, as a result of our experience, that counselling or psychotherapy in general is extremely helpful for most people at some time in their lives. Often the harsh conflicts that arise in families are appropriate occasions for parents to come to some understanding of their own unresolved needs and conflicts. Societal values and styles of child-rearing may be at fault, but the most appropriate place for individuals to begin to gain such understanding is in their own lives.[5]

Awareness of the child's impressionability at this vital stage of development can create much anxiety in conscientious parents desirous of bringing up their children in the healthiest possible way. It may be consoling to remember that children have been reared for hundreds of thousands of years and, barring serious deprivation or severe trauma, have grown up reasonably healthily. Love and attention, together with consistent and considered values are the hallmarks of 'good enough' parents at this and all other stages.

4   LATER CHILDHOOD

5–11 years   Shakespeare: The whining schoolboy with his satchel
                          And shining morning face, creeping like snail
                          Unwillingly to school.

Freud: Latency period.
Erikson: Industry versus inferiority.

In Freudian language this is the 'latency period' — a time when sexual and aggressive urges are repressed, to be released in full force in adolescence. From our own observation, however, it would seem that neither sexuality nor aggression is completely repressed. It seems, rather, that the constrictions of school, home and society generally prevent much in the way of expression of those urges, but that they are consciously active within.

This stage is decisive on so many counts, for it is when the child learns to work — or to slack. Many do derive satisfaction from the feeling of having produced a good piece of work which has been valued and openly appreciated. Lack of encouragement, or unhelpful comparisons, can result in strong feelings of inadequacy, and in the pointlessness of effort.

Now he is learning from other people who may be vastly different from his parents. These new mentors may have different values, different views, different sartorial standards, and this can create conflict. Up to now parents have been regarded as the model for all behaviour, in addition to being omnipotent and omniscient. Coping with this conflict may, temporarily, hold up the learning process in some thoughtful and sensitive children. Once diversity has been accepted as part of life, then they are on their way to maturity.

At this stage the average child is very curious. He wants to know about his environment — what makes things happen the way they do. There are so many mysteries that he wants to fathom, and how his questions are answered is all-important. No parent or teacher can have all the answers, but all questions need to be seriously accepted and considered. These answers should always be truthful, though in some areas — such as the sexual — it may be wise not to go beyond what is asked at the time (during the early stage), and to ascertain before answering at all, what the child already knows and thinks. He is likely to have his own fantasies that will need exploring and correcting.

For a child to learn effectively his early experiences of the world must not have been too damaging, and this experience depends largely upon the treatment he has received from his mother or mother-surrogate, very early on. Where there has been disruption, for any reason, of his emotional development in that early phase, it may be reflected in his slowness or complete inability to learn. If life has gone smoothly and his world (mainly his mother) has been friendly, consistent and responsive, then from now on the child is free to progress naturally step by step.

It is during this latency stage that learning disorders may begin to show, usually in reading, spelling, numeracy and writing. Most children who are referred to counsellors have learning disorders or, at least, some measure of under-achievement.

Much anxiety is experienced unnecessarily because of too rigid expectancy of uniformity and consistency of development in children of this and other stages. The fact is that there is great natural variability between children, and among the various areas of development in a single child. Some children may be precocious in one way, and backward in another. Unless this fact is recognised, fully accepted and acted upon, then grave damage can result.

Adrienne was an attractive, though over-weight seventeen year old who came seeking help to handle her feelings of guilt and unworthiness. She felt that in some way she had special power over people, and that this power was evil. When asked to specify, she spoke of one of the girls at school who was very able, and who seemed to excel in every subject. One day when they were in the gymnasium, and this clever girl was walking along the beam perfectly poised, Adrienne wished fervently that she would fall, *and she did.* It was an awkward fall and the girl broke her collarbone. A few complications meant that she suffered a lot and took months to recover. For this Adrienne blamed herself.

From early days she showed great musical prowess. Piano, violin, clarinette, all seemed natural vehicles for her talent. Rapidly she out-stripped her musical contemporaries, and was considered something of a genius.

Her special instrument was the violin and every year, in addition to routine examinations which she always passed with distinction, she entered public competitions and invariably won first prize.

Because of her brilliance in the realm of music, she was expected to be outstanding in all other subjects when, in fact, she was simply average or below. This created tension at school, home, and within the girl herself. She did not pass the eleven-plus examination, so her parents paid for her to go to a private Grammar School. In spite of all contrary evidence, expectations remained high for general academic achievement to match musical ability. She broke down under the strain. Anger, fear, envy, and the feeling of being loved and valued only for her musical talent, not for herself, built up within until she could no longer cope.

Her violin, which now she loathed and could not bear to touch, was put away. Her deep love for music turned to hatred. Now she saw her gift as evil, and the gymnasium incident confirmed it for her.

That is an illustration of the devastating effect of insistent expectation of consistency of achievement in every aspect of development. Sometimes all-round performance happens: more frequently it does not. Why it should be so, we do not know. Perhaps there is a greater degree of variability built into some people's genetic codes. Whatever the reason, the fact remains.

During these school years the child finds himself able, for the first time, to make real friendships which are meaningful to him. Through these friendships he is able to validate himself and his own deep feelings — to test himself out with them and against them — and to form a working hypothesis about himself, siblings, his peers, his parents, teachers and others. When he has reached this satisfactory stage of development — of self/other affirmation — he is ready to begin risking the hazard of leaving childhood behind and taking the next step — into adolescence.

5 ADOLESCENCE

11–20 years   Shakespeare: . . . and then the lover
                             Sighing like furnace with a woeful balad
                             Made to his mistress' eyebrow.

Freud: Puberty.
Erikson: Identity versus Identity diffusion.

Launching into this stage is sometimes likened to the birth trauma. The lucky few slide through almost painlessly, while most struggle through, kicking and protesting. It is an important watershed in the developmental process.

The journey from babyhood to adolescence is a long and interesting one, full of challenging experiences. Nowadays, physical maturing begins around the eleventh year — sometimes even earlier — and can continue until the early twenties. Alongside physical growth goes intellectual development and varying degrees of emotional instability often show themselves. Conflicts of early childhood tend to rise again in more urgent and dramatic form. Character and personality are being confirmed visibly — early 'pencilling in' is now being boldly over-written. Wise, thoughtful handling is needed.

There are three specific areas of dramatically rapid growth: intellectual, emotional and social.

Intellectual growth can be spasmodic. Physical changes sometimes interfere with mental activity, holding it up or speeding it on. Because of rapid growth and development the teenager, at times, seems tired, apathetic and listless, but at other times is spurred on to lively intellectual creativity. Very often learning proceeds at a phenomenal rate, and it is at this time that differences are most marked and special aptitudes show themselves.

Ideally, by this time he will have learned to work by himself as well as with others, and in the process have gained some confidence and competence. The fortunate ones who have felt loved 'for nothing', as it were, can now add 'earned approval' to their experience, and this can be exhilarating. The less fortunate may feel it necessary to work and succeed *in order* to be loved, and this can result in debilitating anxiety.

If he has found difficulty in learning, his much earlier self-image may have taken a beating. If he started well but, somehow, fell by the wayside, he may try to restore the image by being excessively good, i.e. approved of by seeking to curry favour; or excessively bad, i.e. disapproved of by wilful, delinquent behaviour. This could affect the way he relates to a future partner, so needs careful monitoring.

Emotional strain and stress is the inevitable accompaniment of unusually rapid growth and change. The hitherto chatty, cheerful child is often transformed into the moody, morose teenager — difficult to live with and a puzzle to himself and his parents. He needs help and knows it, yet cannot bear to accept it when offered. He is often offensively critical, and turns away from the family standards which have been his own until now. Parental authority is anathema, and he does his best to flout it. All this is irksome, to say the least, but it is natural and represents normal development.

It is vital for the older adolescent to move out from under the parental umbrella which has sheltered and protected him all his life. During childhood he has, to some extent, seen his parents as models of perfections. In adolescence his illusions are shattered. He now perceives his parents as ordinary human beings with flaws and weaknesses. This is a distressing but necessary shock which, if received with a reasonable measure of tolerance, should lead to the acceptance of reality — the 'good enough' reality. There is profit as well as loss.

Social growth is sometimes characterised in adolescence by a special attachment to an older man or woman — a kind of hero-worship or 'crush'. In the young person who is developing healthily and normally this is a transitional phase — the transfer of feeling from parent to a new love-object — and as such may be wholly salutary.

Friendship with the opposite sex at this stage is often of a romantic, superficial and transitory nature, though in some cases it can be deep and enduring. The ostensible reason for adolescent boys and girls gathering together may be intellectual or athletic pursuits, but the sex element is always present, even when not explicit.

Much of the trying behaviour of the adolescent is due to emotional growing pains. He is arrogantly self-opinionated in a way that is hard to take, but this is generally because he *feels* ignorant. He is often irritatingly boastful, because deep down he *feels* inadequate. At his most maddening he is, in fact, simply an ordinary human being, like his parents, but with special problems which need to be seen in the context of normal human growth and development.

What he needs most of all is consistent love. He also needs plenty of freedom, with limited responsibility. Too much responsibility can be oppressive when he has so much else to contend with, but too little can inhibit growth. He needs sufficient money to prevent him from feeling deprived, but not an excessive amount. When he is reticent and withdrawn, this should be respected and accepted. Unless he asks for advice, it should be offered only occasionally and then sparingly. Too much discipline will be resented and, in most cases, kicked against.

Before the beginning of this stage sex instruction needs to have been given. Discussion with peers are a serious and important part of the adolescent's life, and it is valuable if these can be augmented occasionally by discussion with adults concerning sex, love and marriage, birth-control, abortion, parenting, etc., so that in the airing of opinions and views there is some opportunity for the correcting of misinformation and false ideas.

The adolescent is caught between two worlds and, being human, he wants the best of both. He is pressurised to give up being a child, and part of him wants this more than anything else, but another part still wants the cushioning of childhood, and he fears the transition.

Being now physically equipped and having bewildering sexual urges and drives he is told that he must not have sexual experience until he is 'grown up'. This is like Santa Claus leaving a note on a child's toys to the effect that they must not be played with until the summer holidays.

The teenager does not understand himself, his parents, his teachers, or other adults, so he is often moody, edgy and generally difficult. He wants and needs to be with friends who are passing through the same sort of experience. But even this has snags because he has an intense desire to be on a par with his friends in every aspect of their development. So when he notices differences, he becomes anxious. He may hear that some of the boys have started shaving, when he has not. In the changing rooms he might discover that some of the boys have bigger penises than he has. An adolescent girl may note and be told that some of her friends are wearing bras when she is not; or they are not, when she is. She may feel fat and ugly or feminine and attractive.

Generally there is a great need to conform to the appearance and behaviour of peers, and too great a difference in any way can create immense anxiety. 'Am I normal?' or 'Do you think I'm under-sexed because I don't feel as the others say they do?' are questions they ask in embarrassed desperation.

There is frequently a period of depression in adolescence. After all, it is a kind of bereavement period. He is mourning lost childhood. He wants to be grown up, yet it is grieving and scaring to let go of familiar childhood. Apathy and despair may descend upon him, and sadly this is sometimes mistaken for sheer laziness. At this point he may find it easier and safer to withdraw from his group altogether, being plagued by agrophobic feelings of fearing to go out of the house, or even from his own room.

It he does go to school his fear of failure can be overwhelming. Many adolescents are *told* not to worry at crucial examination time. 'If you fail it won't be the end of the world'. But because of other messages received along childhood's way, they *feel* that love and acceptance depend upon success. They stand to lose everything. At this time, therefore, anger, depression, destructiveness, over-eating, starving, addiction, suicide attempts, are strands in the adolescent behaviour pattern that are not incongruous. They have a sad logic of their own.

There is so much to cope with during this long phase that turbulence is normal. Adjusting to rapid growth rate can be quite disturbing. The boy is awkward and embarrassed by his clumsiness. He has nocturnal emissions, and unless he has been prepared for them can find them worrying and frightening.

Girls often become self-conscious about their developing breasts, and about menstruation. If they have not been informed and prepared for this latter development, distress and fear is likely to result in an unhelpful attitude towards this monthly event throughout her life.

As we have said, the need to conform is at this time stronger than ever before; not with parents, teachers, or other adults as was the case in childhood, but with peers. Hair-styles, dress, smoking, drinking, 'pot', are some of the areas where there is often pressure. Popularity and acceptance with other young people is what matters most. If he is lucky enough to find satisfaction, acceptance, and security with a group which does not smoke, take drugs, or behave extravagantly, then he is likely to identify with them happily, and behave similarly.

Two disturbing aspects of this pressing need to conform with the group, come what may, are:

(1) those who are different are often distrusted and even hated;
(2) it is easy to be trapped into an inappropriate life-style which then becomes permanent.

Adolescence can be a perilous time. At some point during this stage, fantasy and imagination give way to interaction and exploration of the world and other people. This is particularly true in the sexual area. It nearly always leads to masturbation. Self-stimulation which seems to be a normal part of this stage of development, still evokes feelings of guilt and anxiety, needlessly.

Anxiety and guilt on this score turn some young people in the direction of the counselling-room, but it may take time to tease out the real reason for their coming.

A brief period of homosexual feelings and behaviour is fairly common during adolescence, but this does not usually lead to adult homosexuality. Emotionally humans are not so much heterosexual or homosexual but, in varying degrees, bisexual. This can be illustrated by reports that 80% of women who before going to prison were exclusively heterosexual, became involved in exclusively homosexual relationships while there. Also, in an all-male seminary of twelve hitherto completely heterosexual students, within two years eight were engaged in homosexual activity.

Heterosexual exploratory activity goes on, too. Few adolescents are ignorant about sex these days, *but some are*. All need to be aware of the consequences of sexual behaviour; that 'petting' and 'necking' can lead to intercourse, even when it was not originally intended. Parents cannot take it for granted that their children 'know it all'.

At this stage exploration is rarely purely investigatory or for learning purposes only. Emotions, motives and drives are mixed and complex. 'Getting back' at parents can be a conscious or unconscious reason for allowing sexual exploration to 'get out of hand'.

> Fifteen year old Doreen came from a very restrictive, respectable, anxiety-ridden, Presbyterian home. From the day menstruation began her mother watched her like a hawk. Every move was monitored, friends vetted and arrangements scrutinised. The longing to break out was intense and pressing, so when a boy at school invited her to his home in his parents' absence she accepted with alacrity and went nervously but, in her own words, 'as though in answer to an urgent call'. The call to hit back?
>
> Pregnancy, followed by abortion, brought pain and suffering to all concerned. She came for counselling because her violent feelings were terrifying her. She still had the urge to 'hit out', and did so frequently — kicking furniture, banging doors, damaging paintwork in and outside of the home. Hatred of her mother frightened her most of all. She felt *bad*. Sometimes she 'planned' a violent death and deliberately walked into traffic, but survived without injury.

Adolescents need acceptance and esteem from parents and other adults but, it seems, most of all from their contemporaries. This is essential to healthy psychological growth. They may not always want, but they certainly need authority which is exercised with reason and intelligent understanding of the changes and confusions going on within. Frank discussion with regard to sanctions and rules is included in 'authority'. Encouragement to cross the bridge from dependence to independence is another need. If parents and other adults can help him to do this with growing confidence, responsibility and self-reliance, then they are making a valuable contribution to the emergence of a new adult.

6   YOUNG ADULTHOOD

20s–30s   Shakespeare: . . . Then a soldier
                      Full of strange oaths and bearded like the pard . . .
                      Seeking the bubble reputation
                      Even in the cannon's mouth.

Freud: Genitality and later stages of individuation.
Erikson: Intimacy versus isolation.

The new man or woman has, if all has gone reasonably well, successfully negotiated the identity-crisis and has emerged with a strong wish to fuse this partially affirmed identity with others. It must be rare indeed for the resolution of identity to be achieved fully in adolescence, for it is a life-long search. There are those who do not maintain the search and then they, to all intents and purposes, cease to live; but for the new 'alive' adult there comes the need for intimacy. At the same time, he is often afraid to come out from his essential privacy. Erikson regards this stage of development as the time when the battle between intimacy and isolation is fought out. Implicit in the concept of intimacy is the ability and willingness to commit oneself to a relationship.

Every relationship is a facet of the real self, and the young adult needs an underlying value system to bring together all the roles he plays within a relationship. A role is a particular activity in relation to other people, but when he has found a personal patterning of these, and confirmed that it is satisfying, then he experiences a sense of wholeness and wellbeing. This 'bringing together' becomes his adult identity, which is essentially personal and private. The finding and achieving of this integration is not a straightforward or simple matter — it can take many years — and indeed eludes some people altogether.

There are pressures from within and without to prepare for the future which seem to deny, at least temporarily, this urgent need for intimacy. For some this conflict is no more than a brief skirmish, with the outcome scarcely ever in doubt, but for others it assumes the proportions of a full-blown and costly battle.

It is not always easy to distinguish between a real need to prepare for the future, and the avoidance of intimate commitment. The 'perpetual student' who goes from one course to another, never committing himself to job or people, is an example of this kind of avoidance. Very often he does not know what he is preparing himself for, but it is a socially acceptable way of opting out of commitment.

The rationale behind this kind of extended preparation, or lengthy period of travel, exploration or experiment before settling down, can be altogether sound; but even when it is not a commitment-avoidance ploy, it can become a way of life that is self-limiting.

Don and Betty seem very much in love. Their relationship is relaxed and mutually nourishing when they are together. Both are professional people in dissimilar spheres. With reasonable sacrifice on both sides marriage would be possible, but neither's sacrifice is acceptable to the other on quite 'reasonable' grounds. Simply living together is considered untenable for the same 'sound' reasons.

Don repeatedly and unnecessarily accepts archaelogical assignments which take him out of the country for periods of up to two years at a time. Betty takes on concurrent research projects. Their reunions are ecstatic and temporarily satisfying.

They are intelligent and well-informed people and may actually be aware of the name of the game they are playing, i.e. intimate-commitment-avoidance, but they continue with it.

Betty is very unhappy: Don seems content, at present, with his 'spectator sport'.

The young adult who follows his stronger urge for intimacy will, ultimately, be led to thoughts of marriage or some form of permanent or long-term commitment. During adolescence he will most likely have been through a number of one-to-one relationships, each contributing something to him, but of relatively fleeting interest. Then comes a relationship of a different calibre, one out of which he does not grow. One that increasingly supplies his needs. This time he wants to commit himself. This person belongs in his private world in a way that no one else ever has. Eventually they unite — physically and emotionally holding each other tightly, comfortably and securely. This has something in common with the mother and baby relationship, but there are vast differences.

In this way, marriage is a second time round, starting with a kind of infancy. We know the basic needs and wants of babies and, intrinsically, lovers need and want the same. Eric Rayner says:

> What deeply gratifying experiences can marriage provide that other more transient relationships do not? . . . The individual can feel valued above all others by someone else. This stimulates his functioning, just as a baby is enhanced by being loved. What is more, by reciprocating this he is not overburdened with guilt. There is also being cared for and watched over by the equivalent of a watchful parent who alleviates anxiety . . .
> It seems that many people look for trustworthiness and sympathy as the prime values in a spouse over and above all others . . . As far as these primitive yearnings are concerned, time and age count for little, for the adult still feels them.[6]

At this second time round point, though, they are affected by what happened to them the first time round. They cannot remember it consciously, of course, but memory is alive in the unconscious, and expresses itself either as feelings of confidence and wellbeing, or of anxiety and fear that the good life may not be what it seems, and might go sadly wrong at any time.

Young adults may approach marriage with unreasonable expectations. Fear may foster commitment-anxiety so that at the last moment one or the other gets 'cold feet' and escapes before being trapped. Unrealistic hopes may lead to bitter disillusionment.

Just as the baby has to settle for the 'good enough' mother, the adult needs to be able to settle for the 'good enough' partner. This is not falling out of love, but a move out of the realm of fantasy into reality. A young couple can bring individual independence together and unite as equal partners in intimate interaction.

This intimate relationship needs to be worked at, nurtured and guarded against unwarranted intrusion. If one or other of the partners has not satisfactorily emerged from the oedipal crisis, then this intimate relationship may be seriously threatened. In *Emotional Problems of Living*, English and Pearson say:

> We all know men . . . who have emotional ties to their mothers which they

cannot break or relinquish. They do not marry, or if they do, they have an unsatisfactory marriage because they are trying to be a lover to two women — the wife and the mother. The result usually is that such a man satisfies neither woman and is himself in great conflict over his feelings for each.[7]

Responsible, intimate commitment pre-supposes maturity, and if the necessary emotional break from mother or father has not been made, it is better for the young adult to postpone commitment.

When Jennifer and John came to tell of their decision to start divorce proceedings after nine years of marriage, the intimacy had already gone from the relationship together with the commitment. Their firm intention and desire at the start had been that of a permanent intimate commitment, but intrusion, in the form of John's mother, had been allowed, insidiously, to erode this commitment.
John, an only son, born when his father was away on a long-term Civil Service assignment, was brought up by mother alone for three years. The umbilical cord, emotionally speaking, was never broken. Neither could separate from the other. Jennifer always felt an outsider.
She hoped that the birth of their daughter would bring about a change in the triangular relationship, and restore the intimacy to which she was committed and entitled, but in spite of agonising battles the child, too, was absorbed by John's mother, and Jennifer remained the spectator.
Now, without nutriment, the relationship has withered and died of starvation.

If all goes well, and the desire for parenthood is mutual, the union of the two young adults may result in a child whose advent and presence can be the means of enriching the relationship, or impoverishing it.
The birth of a baby is usually a joyous event, but it cannot be joyful all the time. Strains, inconvenience, exhaustion, anxiety, feeling tied and restricted can, for some, take the immediate pleasure out of life. If each supports the other at this time, then the relationship is likely to survive intact, but if not is at serious risk.
Their capacity for parenthood is, inevitably, related to their own experience of being parented. Generally speaking, they will pass on what they have received. Some, however, having become aware of the deprivation they suffered, determine to be better parents than their own. They may then try too hard and set themselves an unrealistic goal, so introducing further strain.
The husband may have been mothered by his wife in the early stages of their marriage, but now she has a real baby and needs his help and support, i.e. she now needs to be 'fathered' herself. This switch of roles is very difficult for many men to effect, and some never manage it. It is a crucial time.
Mother might find her need for love being met by the baby, and if father is left out he may be tempted to look beyond the marriage. Many marriage difficulties are triggered by this situation.
During these strenuous years, it can seem that active parenthood will last for ever. In one sense it should: in another it should not. Children grow up and need to be 'let go'. In the above illustration it is clear that John's mother was unwilling or unable to 'let go' because of her own desperate needs.

At this time a period of quiet reflection, and an assessment of life so far, can be of value, giving confidence to go ahead and face 'the mid-life crisis'.

7 MIDDLE-AGE

40s–50s   Shakespeare: . . . and then the justice
                    full of wise saws and
                    murderous instances . . .
            Erikson: Generativity versus self-absorption.

'The young look forward; the old look backward; the middle-aged look startled!' Forty is said to be the old age of youth, and fifty the youth of old age. Biologically middle-age begins in the middle and late thirties, but when the forty mark is reached, then it is official! The Spanish call it the age of metal — silver in the hair, gold in the teeth, and lead in the feet! 'The hard part of life', said Mark Rutherford, 'is neither the beginning nor the end, but the long, dull stretch that lies between.'

Middle-age, then, is a distinct phase of human development and maturation with specific characteristics and unique problems and needs. Dr. Brice Pitt writes:

> The phrase 'mid-life crisis' refers to an anxious search for a personal identity after what seems to be years of playing roles for others. WHO AM I? A husband, wife, father, mother, son, daughter, employer, employee, housewife, butcher, baker, candle-stick maker, voter, tax-payer, rate-payer, tenant, house-owner — but WHAT am I to ME? What have I done with my life? Where am I going? Why? Panic over unrealised ambitions, the awful feeling that life is unlikely to alter much, the trapped sense that 'this is it' occasionally lead to drastic changes of career . . . or of partner . . . which leave the world stunned. This usually means that there was unfinished business from an earlier crisis, say the original quest for identity in adolescence, to add fuel to the flames of middle-aged conflict. Past fears denied, longings suppressed, decisions postponed are now resolved in an epic or catastrophic upheaval which attempts to throw off the past, wipe the slate clean and create a new person. Needless to say, the gamble often fails.[8]

Each period of life has its own particular positive aspects. *Childhood* is the formative period. *Adolescence* leads to self-consciousness and is the time for decisions, ideals, ambitions, vitality, anticipation, and the awakening of love. In *middle-age* the man (or woman) often feels settled, comfortable in his home. Children may still be a full or partial responsibility. It can be a dangerous time when zeal and enthusiasm wane or evaporate altogether. At this time ambitions and hopes of youth come up against stark reality. Some prizes might have been won along the way, but somehow they may not seem all that glittering now.

At this stage he is, as Jung said, 'in the firm grip of nature'. Often his responsibilities increase and extra sacrifices are demanded of him. The children's education may be of compelling importance, yet at the same time he feels the need to look carefully at his own career. There are so many anxieties many of which have to be suppressed in order that he may function at a reasonable level. But nerves may be on edge, and it is at this stage that husband/wife may feel they need more than each other to keep life interesting or tolerable. Life can seem a deadly routine.

Because of this, there may be a temptation to recklessness, and in some cases, to counter this, a complete change may have a steadying effect. It is certainly a time for re-assessment, and perhaps adjustment.

An awareness that half of life is over can be depressing and anxiety-making. The 'middle-ager' may become discouraged and disappointed at having left no visible tracks so far. A need for new goals is experienced, and he may find it desirable to transfer his interest which had been centred in things, to people.

During his twenties and early thirties all his energies have been given to establishing himself and, usually, his family, and to consolidating his own position. Everything at a deep level within himself, which seemed not to be relevant to those objectives, was neglected and repressed. This can apply to childhood memories and character traits. It may account for some of the bewilderment experienced by parents who sometimes begin to wonder if they have just imagined the past!

But at the onset of middle-age, it is more difficult to give the psychic energy necessary to hold down these parts of himself, and they tend to surface painfully. As in adolescence, unexpected and often unprepared for changes occur within him.

There is some gradual change in sexuality, and the fear of impotence can become a crippling obsession; the fear actually creating the problem. This unbridled fear can propel the middle-ager towards extra-marital sexual activity — a kind of 'testing out' in what might appear more stimulating conditions. But the anxiety engendered increases the possibility of impotence. He needs to be reassured that, all else being equal, his sexual life can remain active and satisfying well into old age.

Marriage relationships benefit from being reassessed, and new ways found of improving the loving shared between them. At some time during this period the woman will recognise early signs of the menopause. This whole process is negotiated by many with relative ease, but others anticipate it with dread, and experience considerable physical and emotional discomfort. There is medical help available to deal with physical symptoms, and although the psychological spin-off is not so easily handled, good counselling/therapy can enable her to cope.

By this time children are becoming increasingly independent, and leaving home for university, college, or to share a flat with friends. All too often mother's sense of identity goes with the children. She does not quite know who she is. She feels redundant and uncared for. For one reason or another she may be plagued by feelings of having failed as a mother, and then has a sense of not having 'lived' at all. Panic may set in, sometimes leading to wild attempts to recapture her youth. Hopefully she can be helped to face the problem of 'unlived' life and lost opportunities, and also to give up what she can never now have.

Physical attractiveness is always important to a woman, and at this time she may feel she is losing out. As the mirror reflects the odd wrinkle or grey hair her sense of 'lost youth' is painful. Permission to grieve over this real sense of loss may be what she needs. When that is properly done there can be a readiness to discover what life has to offer; to accept serenely the 'good enough' life and, to her surprise, she may find it very good indeed.

In early middle-age there is often an indecisiveness because of fear; a withdrawal, or at the other extreme, an extravagant 'acting out', for the same reason. There is no more propitious time for taking advantage of the kind of self-exploration that a counsellor/therapist, or a peer group can offer. Where reality has not been seriously looked at and coped with during this period, the resulting depression can lead to utter despair.

In Arthur Miller's play, *Death of a Salesman*, from which we quoted earlier, Willy Loman the salesman, is summed up by his son, Biff. 'He had the wrong dreams. All, all wrong. He never knew who he was.'

In middle-age the fact of having had the 'wrong' dreams may have to be faced. Willy Loman's dreams were day-dreams which turned his proper dreams into nightmares. In his early days Loman had been a success. He seemed well-placed in the rat race. But when men race like rats they tend to lose themselves. Willy refused to face facts about himself or his sons. Desperately he wanted Biff to follow in his footsteps, thus perpetuating himself, although it was clear he should have been a farmer. As a salesman Biff was a dead loss, but Willy drove him on.

Willy lived on hire purchase, gathering possessions frantically, and the instalments drained more than his bank-balance. 'Once in my life', he said, 'I would like to own something before it is broken! I'm always in a race with the junk-yard.' Willy's only friend said to him one day, 'The only thing you've got in this world is what you can sell.' In a sense not intended this cynical statement is true. The only real possession is the self and, particularly in middle-age, it is very easy to put it up for sale. 'Wrong dreams' drove Willy to suicide, but he really died years before his death.

So, middle-age is yet another period of transition and, if at the end of it personal and interpersonal work has been done reasonably successfully and a way of integrating the philosophical and spiritual meaning of work, possessions, and position in life has been found, then it is possible for him to settle down to enjoying life as it is. He may then be free to add new interests to it, deploying new skills, knowledge and discovered gifts in a different way. This often is a 'season of mellow fruitfulness'.

8 THE ELDERLY

60s–80s   Shakespeare: . . . the lean slipper'd pantaloon with spectacles on
                      nose and pouch on side . . .
              Erikson: Integrity versus Despair.

'Age is a state of mind', read the graffiti on a station waiting-room wall, to which a wag (or perhaps a nettled 60+) had added, 'and of the legs and the back'.

To some extent the stereotype of the elderly as being sick, fixed in ideas, helpless, hapless, unable to learn or work, is being forced out of existence by the vigorous life-style of so many of those who qualify, chronologically, for this designation.

All the same, the life cycle does proceed inexorably. There is, without doubt, some diminution of physical strength and energy. Muscles show signs of a certain slackening of purpose; eyesight is not what it was, and often the same goes for hearing. Most disturbing of all, memory begins to play tricks, and notepad and pencil become essential impedimenta to be carried around, otherwise many day to day matters slip out of mind. Ordinary everyday words (and names) which have been part of the vocabulary for a lifetime, refuse to surface when bidden. This can be unnerving, especially for those who continue to engage in public speaking or group-discussion etc. Fear of this happening worsens the condition, creating mental blocks that have nothing directly to do with the ageing process.

The counselling-room sees some of this age-group panicked by signals received which seem to be indicating the imminent end of dignified, self-respecting and meaningful living. A quiet unhurried look at facts, as well as at fears and feelings, can sometimes restore equilibrium to an elderly life which has been temporarily off-balance.

A release from guilt-feelings can be a compensation for diminishing vitality in the person whose inner commands of 'ought, must and should' have been experienced as tyrannical. It is no longer possible to carry them out. Now this person is in the position to relax into unambitious contentment. The dangers of doing this too soon or too completely are obvious.

Some of the fears expressed at this time of life are based on facts. There are some elderly people who have to face the upheaval of change — uprooting themselves from the place in which they have lived for many years — because the house is tied to the job, and retirement means relinquishing it, or for family reasons. There are anxieties of living on a pension for the first time in their lives. What if they can't manage? The fear of insecurity. The fear of being compelled by circumstances or relatives to go into a home, is very real for some.

Most prevalent of all is the fear of losing dignity. There is also fear of becoming isolated, of losing significant relationships, colleagues, neighbours who have become close friends; and fear of not being able or willing to make new ones.

Often elderly folk feel they are no longer needed by anyone, so work of any kind is pointless and valueless. This fear of being of no use is very real. There are a few who do enjoy being dependent — perhaps because the desire to behave in an infantile way has been held in check since childhood and, now that they have been told they are in 'second childhood', the necessity for restraint is removed. But for most people the fear of being dependent is unnerving. To some sons and daughters, alas, power over parents brings a measure of relief because, consciously or unconsciously, it is experienced as 'poetic justice', 'table-turning' or 'chickens coming home to roost'. This is a fearful situation.

For many there is the fear of death itself. The intensity of the fear varies. Belief in life after death brings comfort to some, but to those whose creed has implied a vengeful God, this can add to their terror.

It is important that there should be the opportunity of expressing and exploring fears and anxieties with someone who is trusted, as well as to pursue activities and interests, as far as possible, which will enrich the whole person. There are certainly losses which have to be accepted, whether churlishly or graciously, but there are undoubted gains. Seward Hiltner in his book, *Self-understanding* says:

> Except in a few rare illnesses the ability to learn declines only very slowly with advancing years. Sexual capacity continues into older years. Senility is not a disease but a period of life. The proportion of crippling or disabling illnesses among older people is not much higher than it is among the middle-aged . . . Medicine is developing a new speciality of geriatrics, and is gaining skill in helping people to prepare their bodies for effective functioning in later years. The losses most feared are for the most part those which are with intelligent action most avoidable.[9]

9   OLD-AGE, DYING, AND DEATH

80 plus   Shakespeare: Sans teeth, sans eyes, sans taste, sans everything.

When Adenaur, the German President, was unwell and his doctor said to him, 'I can't make you young again', Adenaur replied, 'I don't want to be made young again; all I want is to go on getting older'.

Perhaps more old people in their final stage agree with Swift's words 'Everyman deserves to live long, but no man would be old'. Jacques, in Shakespeare's 'As you like it' possibly expresses the fears of the majority:

> Last scene of all in this eventful history
> Is second childishness and mere oblivion
> Sans teeth, sans eyes, sans taste,
> Sans everything.

A frightening image.

The very old person's increased or complete dependence on others is real, not imaginary, and life is genuinely difficult. His intellectual and emotional resources may be drained, and he may no longer be able to arrange and organise his daily routine. There are those who manage to keep alert, active and happily useful to the end, but for most there are problems.

An understanding of the person's 'strategies of adjustment' and psychological defences can be useful when looking for a way of giving support at this time and, indeed, help may have to be limited to the handling of specific problems as they arise, over a short period.

It is essential to recognise the individuality of the old person, and to take account of the past. In some Eventide Homes for Salvation Army Officers it is general policy to encourage the residents to don their uniform once a week — usually Sunday night — so that they can remind themselves, each other, and the staff of what they have been and still are, and of their individual contribution to life. There are some negative aspects to this procedure, but overall the psychological effect is beneficial.

In her book, *Old Age in the Modern World*, Margery Fry writes: 'To the administrator an individual may be just "that old woman, I think her name is

Jones", but to herself she is the Katey Jones who won a prize for scripture, and had the smallest waist in the class, with a thousand other distinctive features, who just happens to be old.'

Differences in the young, middle-aged and elderly are more easily recognisable than in the very old. It is necessary to understand that the very old person is unable to change in any fundamental way. Pressure to do so can only create stress. By the time this stage has been reached flexibility and manoeuvreability have gone.

Respect for the old has a right 'feel' about it. 'Dishonour not the old. We shall all be numbered among them' (*The Apocrypha*) is a salutary maxim. In this area, as in others, children often repeat the pattern of their parents behaviour, therefore, if for no other than purely selfish and utilitarian reasons, a respectful, caring, non-patronising attitude is clearly indicated.

The extrovert at this stage tends to look back to the material successes and failures of the past, whereas the introvert reflects, and is disturbed by what he now sees as his confused thinking throughout life. In retrospective mood the introvert may sometimes be at a disadvantage. His satisfactions in life have been the inner experiences, and when he looks back he may not recall much in the way of external achievement. When he does, he may not value it highly.

Obsessive old people keep checking over incidents in the distant past, worrying over where they might have done better. Others look back and become disturbed when thinking about the consequences of some of their past actions.

Encouragement to look at things in perspective, or simply to let hurtful things go, may be the only positive help that can be given. Where there is a religious belief, and the concepts of forgiveness and commitment in faith are accepted as valid and meaningful, it has been frequently noted that this can bring peace of mind, enabling the old person to face with fortitude whatever future they have.

Death is one of the few remaining taboo subjects in our society today. Few people will talk about it willingly, yet it is the one certainty ahead of us all. Death is part of life, and a good death is a fitting end to a good life.

A general practitioner said recently, 'Most of my patients are trying to pretend they are immortal'. There seems a general conspiracy to banish death from the awareness of the living. The dying are tranquilised and often taken off to hospital. After death the body is put in the hands of strangers for death to be disguised by cosmetics. This, perhaps, is particularly true in the United States of America.

Everyone needs to focus his mind upon death. This helps him to make the transition from starry-eyed youth in which all the doors of opportunity seem open, to the more realistic wisdom of the mature which finds it possible to accept limits without undue frustration and gains hope and satisfaction in continuing to work towards a sound philosophy of life and death.

Medical research may lengthen and make more pleasurable the span of mortality, but death itself can never be overcome. Being human means returning to the soil — 'ashes to ashes; dust to dust'. When man stops ignoring death, and learns to be at ease in its presence, he will live in a healthier and more integrated way. To blot out all thoughts of death is to distort our total way of experiencing the world.

Most, though certainly not all, old people suffer a series of illnesses and growing infirmities before some specific disease takes over and makes recovery impossible. The terminal phase of life then sets in. For the fortunate ones, this may last only a few minutes or hours, as in the case of acute coronary thrombosis. For others as in cancer or motor neurone disease and the like, it may be months.

In this final stage of life it seems that man needs the comforting presence of another human being. At St. Christopher's Hospice in Sydenham, London, two promises are made to patients (all with terminal illnesses); one is that their pain will be removed, and the other that they will not die alone. This takes cognisance of the fact that the fundamental fear is that of pain and loneliness — or is it abandonment?

What is the most helpful attitude towards the dying person? There can be little doubt that it is to be natural. Yet, unless relatives and friends have themselves come to terms with death, it is difficult to be natural — in spite of the fact that death is, like birth, a natural process.

Enforced jollity, in an attempt to cheer up the dying person, is unnatural and unhelpful; similarly, make-believe plans about what he is going to do next year. It is legitimate to sympathise about an old person's pain, but not about his death.

Naturalness is something that comes, and is not learned. If we observe those who give genuine comfort to the dying, it is seen that they themselves are at ease — not anxious. This enables them to be natural because they are not driven into inappropriate attitudes by their own anxiety.

In the cultures where individual life is of small consequence perhaps death, too, is not regarded as a force to be reckoned with. But in western society and culture, in spite of the violence and inhumanity that abounds in some areas, there is a basic reverence for life, and a positive emphasis on the value of the individual. Inevitably, therefore, the thought of surrendering life is cause for anxiety, fear and dread, in varying degrees to most people.

There is need to communicate non-verbally with the dying person. At this stage words are of little use. Perhaps an occasional phrase or two might be useful, but certainly physical contact is of value. Some medical authorities believe that sense of touch is the last to go.

Because of the frequent indignity of incontinence and the feeling of 'being a nuisance', shame can be a stress factor of great dimensions. It is thought, however, that this stress diminishes as the end approaches, and eventually disappears altogether.

In the very last days consciousness is generally dimmed, and interest in life visibly relinquished. In fact, death is *allowed* to come. Premonitions of its approach seem prevalent, though with some these fluctuate, and the dying person may suddenly start behaving as though he expects to recover. It may be that by this temporary denial of death, painful feelings are relieved.

Observation of practising believers, *and* complete atheists, suggests that they seem not to suffer, to the same extent, the anxieties of those who have had *vague* beliefs which have not affected their life-styles.

So death comes — the cycle is complete. All who have been touched, however lightly, by the life that is now over, have imbibed something from him, and to that extent, *at least*, he lives on.

REFERENCES

1. Eric Erikson, 'Eight Ages of Man' in *Readings in Child Behaviour and Development*, edited by C. Stindler, New York, Harcourt, Brace and World, 1964.
   Childhood and Society, New York: Norton, 1967
2. D.H. Stott, 'The Child's Hazards in Utero' In *Modern Perspectives in International Psychiatry*, Edited by John G. Howells, New York, Brunner,/Mazel Publishers, 1971, p.53.
3. Arthur Janov, *The Primal Scream*, & *The Primal Revolution*, Abacus Books, 1976.
4. William Shakespeare, *As You Like it*, Act 2, Scene 7.
5. Leonard Blank and Kenneth Lewes, *Psychology for Everyday Living*, New York, Mayflower Books Inc. 1980, p.18.
6. Eric Rayner, *Human Development*, Allen and Unwin, 1971, p.190.
7. O. Spurgeon English & Gerald H.J. Pearson, *Emotional Problems of Living*. Allen & Unwin, 1968, p.97.
8. Brice Pitt, *Mid-life Crisis*, Sheldon Press, 1980, p.ix.
9. Seward Hiltner, *Self-understanding*, Nashville, Abingdon Press, 1951, p.176.

10   The Counsellor

What kind of a person should the counsellor be? It would be easy to add virtue upon virtue and describe an impossible ideal, but this would be counter-productive. Those readers who have actually met some counsellors would be forgiven for saying, 'How ridiculous!' Others who might be considering the possibility of training to become a counsellor might simply despair, saying, 'If that's the kind of person they're looking for, I haven't a chance.'

Throughout the book there must have been built up in the reader's mind some kind of picture, but simply to bring together strands from previous chapters into some kind of whole could also be disturbing. In one sense, all ideals are frightening. They are also impossible. Realism demands that everyone has the courage of his/her imperfections. Nevertheless, some kind of general consensus as to the kind of person a counsellor should be is desirable and relevant.

Ethel Venables in her book entitled *Counselling*, has a useful paragraph:

> How do we see a counsellor — what sort of person is he? He must first of all have some social skills and be able to establish easy and confident relationships with a client from the outset. He must be able to listen, not only with his ears, but with all his senses, to what this person in distress is conveying to him and he must be able to tolerate the message whatever it is. He must attempt to discriminate between the important issues and the trivial ones, checking back from time to time with the person in front of him that he has got the right message. In this way the client begins a process of sorting and discriminating too and the hope is that he will thus be able to make sensitive and rational decisions about the way ahead[1].

That straightforward description of a good counsellor may not seem too terrifying, but it is still a demanding one. Much of what follows will be an amplification of certain elements in that statement.

Some behaviourists, notably H.J. Eysenck[2], have tried to cast doubts on the effectiveness of 'dynamic' counselling and psychotherapy, and it must be admitted that in this very subjective world it is sometimes difficult to assess the hard evidence beloved of the scientifically minded. The establishing of 'control' groups for the purpose of comparison usually proves impossible. Truax and Carkhuff[3] make the essential point that psychotherapy and counselling lack the required uniformity of content required for experimental assessment.

> To illustrate this point they use a striking simile between counselling and pharmacology. They suggest that research done in the area of 'chemotherapy' would give some strange results if unknown quantities of drugs were given

randomly to some patients and none to others. Yet in counselling research '. . . one group of patients has been given random unknown amounts of various psychological "conditions" collectively labelled "psychotherapy" while another group has received "no psychotherapy".' It would be preferable for experiments in counselling to be set up in a manner similar to pharmaceutical research. The drug (counselling) would be clearly defined, the amount closely measured, and the disease from which the patient suffers carefully diagnosed. If it were possible to delimit any branch of counselling with exactitude and establish with precision the exact problem(s) of the unique client then perhaps some real measurement could take place.[4]

What did emerge, however, when Truax and Carkhuff and others took up the Eysenck challenge was that the results of certain therapists indicated great consistency in the help received by their clients. Following on this, the attempt was made to discover and delineate those elements in the therapist that appeared to facilitate improvement in the client. Thereafter, three characteristics became designated 'core conditions'. The terms used are, *non-possessive warmth, genuineness* and *accurate empathy.*

Every textbook on counselling given space, and every training course on counselling gives time, to a study of these three basic qualities that all counsellors need. So we, too, will seek to define them. Some seem to possess them as a gift of nature, others have to work at them. An interesting, important and encouraging discovery is that to a certain extent they can be acquired.

NON-POSSESSIVE WARMTH

The client does not need heat, he needs warmth. He does not want to be scorched, but comfortable. This is true at the physical level. There should be the right distance between the counsellor and client. If they are too close the client is likely to feel threatened. If they are too far apart, the client may feel abandoned.

But non-possessive warmth applies to the emotional distance between them. Most clients know when this is right. Keeping the correct distance is important throughout. R.D. Laing tells of sitting a long time with a schizophrenic patient and letting his mind wander. The patient asked him why he had 'gone away'. Laing was tempted to deny this and assert his emotional as well as his physical presence, but knew this would be dishonest. So he admitted his failure to 'stay with' the patient, and said that he was back with him now and would try not to leave him again. (This is also an excellent example of 'genuineness' — see next section.)

The warmth must be non-possessive. The counsellor is not taking over the client, even if this is what the latter desires. The expression of the counsellor's positive, loving regard should be experienced as non-threatening. The client must be allowed to breathe; he must not feel 'crowded.'

This 'core condition' is the warmth of an accepting attitude to whatever the client is bringing. He may be experiencing a whole range of feelings — fear, confusion, anxiety, pride, anger, hatred, courage, love — and some of these may be new to him. The counsellor prizes, even cherishes, the client in an unconditional way. His acceptance is non-judgmental.

In order to be able to appreciate people in this creative way, the counsellor needs to find them interesting. 'The longer I live the more do human beings appear to be fascinating and full of interest . . .' wrote Maxim Gorki.[5] He continued, 'Foolish and clever, mean and almost saintly, diversely unhappy — they are all dear to my heart; it seems to me that I do not properly understand them and my soul is filled with an inextinguishable interest in them.' And the people he found particularly interesting were the 'non-achievers'. People 'of a sound mind' were of little interest to him. 'The achieved man, the one perfect like an umbrella does not appeal to me. I am called and doomed, you see, to describe — and what could I say of an umbrella but that it is of no worth on a sunny day?'

Gorki would have made a good counsellor, for counsellors see very few 'achieved' men. Obviously Gorki was interested in men *for their own sake* — and this is important. Those interested in people in order to exercise over them their own power, or to prove a pet theory, are little use as counsellors. Religious people wishing to exploit the emotional needs of an individual in order to 'save' them can also be dangerous. To see the other as a prospective convert does not make for good counselling.

Keith Miller, the American business man converted in middle life, describes in his book *The Taste of New Wine* his own experience. He found that he saw his wife as the 'object' of his Christian witness and this created serious difficulties for them. He writes: 'From the other person's perspective your anxiety to get your "Christian content" across sends out the unspoken message that you have something more important on your mind than him and what he has to say.' So the desire to persuade the client against his will, speaks of a too possessive kind of warmth. Coercion of any kind has no place in counselling.

Non-possessive warmth preserves the client's sense of his own dignity, at the same time creating in him the courage to explore disturbing material within himself. This warmth does not mean weakness. The client's undesirable behaviour may need to be examined, but the person himself is being prized rather than his behaviour.

GENUINENESS

This means an honest relationship *with yourself* — 'to thine own self be true'. Can there be anything more important than self-understanding? How impertinent to try to understand others, and how disastrous it can be to imagine you do, if you are indifferent to the need for self-discovery.

At a conference of marriage-counsellors the question was asked, 'What does a psychiatrist do? The surgeon uses his knife, the physician his drugs. What does the psychiatrist use? The reply given was along the following lines. 'The surgeon uses his knife, but also his personality. He uses his knife scientifically, but his self unscientifically, even if effectively. The physician uses drugs scientifically, but his self unscientifically. The psychiatrist has nothing to use but his own self, but there is this difference — he uses his own self scientifically.'

This seems to us to be a somewhat idealistic view of many psychiatrists today, because they tend to become trapped, through pressure of work, by the medical aspects of their role. But it is certainly true of psychotherapists and counsellors

— the tool they use is themselves. This is why self-scrutiny is an absolute imperative, something that is alien, and even suspect, to ordinary extrovert people.

Whether the word 'scientifically' is the best possible, is open to question. It is certainly the case that the counsellor has no other tool than himself. 'You'd better not compromise yourself, it's all you've got', is advice particularly appropriate to counsellors. He must aim at genuineness.

This necessitates a certain open-mindedness and the ability to accept himself, his 'not-so-good' self as well as his 'better' self. It means the absence of self-deception, teaching him to accept his true nature. There is the need to accept his weaknesses without underestimating his strengths. Bernard Martin argues for this kind of self-acceptance.

To reject oneself, or not to accept oneself, is to be like the card player who refuses to play on the grounds that he has been dealt a bad hand. The good player, on the other hand, is he who can play to the best advantage the cards dealt to him, even if they are only low ones. My education told me that I must change, that I must be or try to be someone else, transform my character. Psychology has taught me to 'play the game', as a good player, in order to make the best use of the cards which life has put in my hands.[6]

This takes courage, for most people safeguard themselves against self-discovery by creating a partially false self-image that is reasonably acceptable. Counsellors are ordinary human beings in this and every other regard, and have their own hide-outs, secret places where they take shelter. This is why analysts must first be analysed, and why most counsellors would be wise to seek some kind of therapy in the interests of their own inner growth. It is why counsellors need to work under supervision.

An additional reason is this: whenever a counsellor tries to penetrate the intimate thoughts of another, in order to discover with him and for him his true condition, he must expect to discover something about himself. Perhaps he will recognise one of his own disguises. Freud is supposed to have said, 'I always feel it is uncanny if I cannot understand the patient in terms of myself'.

The *failure* to recognise shortcomings and weaknesses within himself can become a problem within the relationship. Someone has written: 'The personal counsellor with *unrecognised* problems will project these on to the people coming to him for help, so increasing their confusion. The preacher with *unrecognised* guilt will verbally lash his congregation, inducing unhealthy reactions in young and sensitive people. The social service worker with an *unrecognised* need to feel superior will unconsciously seek to maintain others in a state of dependence.'

Jane's much-loved cat was missing, and the counselling session had perforce to be concentrated on this, to the annoyance of the counsellor. He was not a lover of cats and felt an impatience that he tried to conceal. 'Perhaps', he spoke more abruptly than he intended 'you have to accept the fact that your cat is dead.'

The rest of the session was wasted time. The normal rapport between counsellor and client evaporated. Both experienced disappointment and frustration.

Two factors broke the link between Jane and her counsellor. One was the client's love for her cat with which the counsellor could not empathise. The other was the fact that death was the worst thing the counsellor could imagine, whereas her uncertainty as to whether the cat was alive or dead was, for the client, worse than the thought of death itself. What the counsellor needed to look at within himself was his own attitude to death.

This raises the question as to what the counsellor can do when he does not feel in sympathy with his client. Eric Wood[7] describes the frustration of a group of social workers who were made to feel helpless and hostile by their clients. They felt they were falling short in some way because of their very natural human response. After all, it was their business to care! They needed to learn to accept their hostility and to use it as a pointer to understanding their clients' problems.

Training and experience are the only things that can help here. It is rarely helpful at the beginning of a counselling relationship to express openly and forcefully 'raw' feelings. These may need to be monitored. There does come a time in a longer-term relationship when anger can quite properly be expressed, but even then the way this is done needs to be carefully watched. All the counsellor's feelings can be used to help his understanding of the client's total situation. He must learn to tolerate his own mixed feelings, to understand them, then to use them constructively. Knowing when and what to express and when and what to control is one of the most difficult aspects of the counsellor's art.

What is always essential is this: whatever *is* expressed — although this may not be the whole truth — must be genuine in itself. Samuel M. Natale puts it this way:

> The aim of genuineness in counselling involves the presentation of a non-defensive truthful self in the encounter with the client. It is within the context of genuineness that the patient will be able to test his perceptions of reality. Clinical experience seems to indicate that as we listen to and participate in the world of the client and as we begin to understand the tangled fibres of his experience, we often become more capable of being ourselves. It is frequently the appreciation of the patient's private world which evokes our most positive and genuine responses. Empathy and genuineness are, in effect, simultaneously present. Genuineness precludes facades. It demands honesty.[8]

Should the counsellor become defensive, if he starts playing a role, or hides behind a professional facade, something irretrievable will be lost. What he gives must match his inner experience. This is what facilitates change in the client.

The word 'congruence' is used to describe the absence of pretence, when the counsellor is not putting on a 'front', when he is fully aware of his own feelings and able to live with them and share them when this is appropriate. When he can listen not only to the client, but to himself, and accept the complexity of his feelings without fear.

'Congruence' is an important word in counselling, as it is in life. A well-known television performer, very active in an anti-smoking campaign, was prevailed upon to advertise a certain brand of cigars. He excused himself on the grounds that he owed so much income tax. A perfect example of *in*congruence.

We all know people whom we find it easy to trust from the very start. It is an instinctive response because they are being themselves. We are not dealing with a facade but with the person himself. It is this quality of congruence the client needs from his counsellor.

ACCURATE EMPATHY

Chapter 4 is entitled 'the heart of the matter', and can be read as an exposition of what is meant by the word 'empathy'. The difference between sympathy and empathy has been put succinctly: Sympathy means 'feeling *for*'; empathy means 'feeling *with*'.

Empathy possesses an element that distinguishes it from sympathy, and it is that difference that both counsellor and client need. This difference can be expressed in the two tiny words 'as if'. The following quotation from Samuel Natale explains this:

> In empathy, the counsellor enters into the other person's world and structures the world as the client does. He appreciates the other's world 'as if' it were his own, without ever losing the 'as if' quality. He experiences the person's emotions and fears without being ensnared by them. Because the empathic process involves both identification and objectivity, he is able to experience not only the events which the person encounters but the antecedents and results of those events. Insight is therefore gained. Objectivity is a critical feature of empathy and is, in fact, one of the primary factors that distinguish it from sympathy.[9]

Empathy is the experience of being both inside and outside what the client is sharing. Dag Hammarshold put it this way: 'You can only hope to find a lasting solution to a conflict if you have learned to see the other objectively, but at the same time, to experience his difficulties subjectively.' We are all subjective towards ourselves and everything and everyone else is objective to us. The counsellor, however, learns to share his client's subjectivity, his inner world of thought and feeling 'as if' it were his own, yet he retains a degree of his own objectivity because in the long run that is the client's hope. The client feels the counsellor's sharing of his own experience and is comforted. He also sees that the sharing has not had the demoralising effect on the counsellor as it has had on himself. This is both comfort and challenge. He, the client, need not be overwhelmed.

Way back in 1850, Nathaniel Hawthorne, the American novelist, described in *The Scarlet Letter*, the capacity for empathy possessed by the good doctor:

> If the latter (the doctor) possess native sagacity, and a nameless something more — let us call it intuition; if he shows no intrusive egotism nor disagreeably prominent characteristics of his own; if he has the power, which must be born with him, to bring his mind into such affinity with his patient's that this last shall unawares have spoken what he imagines himself only to have thought; if such revelations be received without tumult, and acknowledged not so often by an uttered sympathy, as by silence, an inarticulate breath, and here and there a word, to indicate that all is understood; if to these qualifications of a

confidant be joined the advantages afforded by his recognised character as a
physician; then, at some inevitable moment, will the soul of the sufferer be
dissolved and flow forth in a dark, but transparent stream, bringing all its
mysteries into the daylight.

This intuitive ability to identify emotionally with others is possessed by many.
They are 'nutritious' people as opposed to 'toxic' people. (It is doubtful that this
capacity is wholly inborn, as Hawthorne suggested. It can, in fact, be cultivated.)
   We are surrounded by people who are desperate for this kind of understanding.
It is estimated that at any one time in every fourth house in any road or street
there is some kind of crisis affecting some member of the household. There is
a frightening world of human need on everyone's doorstep. But most are unaware
until it becomes personal, and many of those who become aware are at a loss
as to how to feel for others, and how to communicate what they do feel.
   There is a pertinent phrase in Alexander Solzhenitsyn's novel, *One Day in
the Life of Ivan Denisovitch*. Throughout the twenty-four hour period described
in the book, Ivan is cold. During the night hours he lies in his cold bed feeling
ill and wondering if his temperature is high enough to get him excused from
duties the next day. In the morning he goes, hopefully, to the health clinic,
which gives him his only contact with warmth. The doctor takes his temperature
and dismisses him. It is not high enough to excuse him from work. As he leaves
the warmth of the clinic, he looks back at the doctor sitting at his desk and asks
the question: 'How can a warm man know how a cold man feels?' How, indeed?
   Empathy means the ability to do just that; being sensitive to another's feelings;
seeing through his eyes; understanding him in his existential situation. 'Sitting
where they sit'. More than this, there needs to be the communication of those
shared feelings. This is not a matter of words only. Hawthorne's doctor receives
revelation 'without tumult', and acknowledges them not by 'an uttered sympathy',
but by 'silence, an inarticulate breath, and here and there a word, to indicate
that all is understood'. Fortunate the patient with such a doctor; fortunate the
client with such a counsellor.
   Our evaluation of other people's experience is usually of a very different
order. We say such things as, 'I understand what is wrong with you', or 'I
understand what makes you behave like that', or 'I, too, have experienced your
trouble but I reacted very differently. Let me tell you . . .'. This is the kind of
'external' understanding we normally offer and receive; an evaluation from the
outside. This does not facilitate change.
   When, however, the client knows that the counsellor does understand *from
within*, and passes no negative judgment, *that* is an emotional climate in which
change and growth become possible. The counsellor acts as an agent for the
client, to help him discover aspects of himself and fragments from the past —
there will be memories and drives, fears and tensions, demands of conscience
and guilt at demands ignored or repudiated. The process is away from chaos
towards psychological and emotional order.
   The client needs to be accurately understood, his conflicts explored and ways
in which the past is active in the present uncovered. The counsellor needs to be
totally available.
   Counselling is a demanding task, and there are many snares and snags. The
counsellor needs to be on the alert for any deterioration in the standard of what

he offers to his clients. We are body/mind entities. Body is always affecting mind, and vice versa. Every reaction is a psychosomatic one. This means that a counsellor's effectivity can be influenced by physical as well as emotional factors. The exhausted counsellor cannot respond to his client, or give to his client, what a rested, relaxed counsellor can. Physical tiredness can result in the drying up of empathy.

Similarly, should the counsellor be passing through a particularly fraught period emotionally, his functioning may be affected. For example, his experience of grieving through the death of a loved one will need to be monitored if he is counselling a similarly bereaved client. His own loss of objectivity can result in an excess of empathy; in fact, his normal empathy may change into a completely subjective sympathy.

Florence was bereaved of her husband and went to a counselling agency for help. Friends were telling her that her grief was becoming morbid. The intake supervisor at the agency who conducted Florence's assessment session, linked this new client with a counsellor who nine months previously had suffered a similar loss. It became clear after three or four sessions that the counsellor had not sufficiently worked through her own grief. The relationship became bogged down; each was increasing the other's distress, so that both needed a different helper.

Any traumatic experience can affect a counsellor's work by robbing him of the insight he needs as to how his attitudes are affecting the client. Emotional instability in the counsellor can cause the client to feel insecure, and he may find himself floundering in consequence. At the other end of the emotional scale, any excessive anxiety in the counsellor can lead to a lack of flexibility in a developing relationship.

It sometimes happens that the counsellor has a succession of 'not-so-good' relationships and becomes demoralised. A serious aspect of this is that he may begin to question the validity of what he has to offer, and this must seriously affect his clients. A client needs — sometimes quite desperately — the confidence of his counsellor in the possibility of improvement in his emotional state. He needs reassurance and, if the counsellor's own conviction has gone, it is bound to register in a negative way.

In addition to the above, there are certain traits generally recognised as likely to lessen a counsellor's effectivity. There is the authoritarian counsellor, who can brook no counter-challenge from the client. There is the passive counsellor who leaves the client to do all the work. There is the detached counsellor whose non-involvement is experienced by the client as rejection. There is the counsellor who needs to play God, and so lessens instead of increases the client's autonomy. There is the perfectionist counsellor, whose demands the client cannot possibly meet.

SUPERVISION

All of this points to the counsellor's own need for ongoing training and supervision. Throughout this book there have been several mentions of supervision. Because of its quite fundamental importance to the counselling scene, some delineating of the supervision process is desirable and necessary.

Supervision consists of regular sessions between a supervisor and counsellor or group of counsellors. The counsellor presents accounts, sometimes with verbatim reports, of his current counselling experience which are then discussed. Good supervision develops into relationship of trust in which open communication is rewardingly easy. The counsellor's reflection on his own work will become increasingly fruitful. The supervisor acts as a facilitator.

The focus of supervision is on learning how the clients can be more effectively helped, and it is in the light of this that the counsellor's own personality may be explored. This borders on personal therapy — and is in practice very often actually therapeutic. But the task-directed character of the supervision must always be borne in mind. It is not therapy as such. In fact, if it becomes clear in supervision that the counsellor stands in need of therapy, then other arrangements should be made.

Louis Marteau writes:

> The function of the supervisor is to help the student increase his skills and develop in the understanding of his own and his client's feelings in such a manner as to increase his sensitivity to and awareness of both. While this relationship is concerned with the emotional development of the student it is not meant to become predominantly therapeutic. Thus the task of the supervisor differs from that of a counsellor, falling between the polarities of counselling and tutoring. Experience in the field, together with a specific academic knowledge of the task would be required of the supervisor.[10]

During recent years various organisations have been formulating procedures leading to the accreditations of supervisors and trainers of counsellors. Some of these are now in actual operation, e.g. The Association for Pastoral Care and Counselling now have a list of accredited trainers and supervisors. The accreditation is for five years only, after which those concerned must apply again and submit themselves to further procedures and assessment. This is to ensure that they have not remained static, but have kept in touch with what has been going on in the field of counselling at the academic, practical and experiential levels.

The accrediting of counsellors is proceeding on similar lines, where the accreditation is also for five years only. It is recognised that so many developments are happening in this field, and the work of counselling is of such crucial importance, there can be no once-for-all accreditation given. Strict control of accreditation is one way in which the rights of clients can be safeguarded. Eventually it will be necessary for state legislation to enter the field of counselling.

Carl Rogers has listed a number of 'characteristics of a helping relationship'. We have found it useful to turn some of these into statements relating to counsellors:

the counsellor needs to be seen as trustworthy;
the counsellor needs to be able to communicate clearly;
the counsellor should be positive in his attitude to the client;
the counsellor needs to be secure enough in himself to allow the client to be separate and different;
the counsellor must be respectful;
the counsellor must be accepting;
the counsellor should not be bound by the client's past or his own past.

In addition to these we would add:
the counsellor needs a gift for listening;
the counsellor needs to understand normal human development;
the counsellor should have sufficient understanding of mental abnormality to know when referral is necessary;
the counsellor should have had training in self-awareness;
the counsellor should be working under supervision.

In case readers feel that this chapter does, in fact, present the picture of an impossible — and therefore demoralising — ideal, we would like to bring it to an end with a statement of H.H. Strupp:

> It seems that there is nothing esoteric or superhuman about the qualities needed by a good therapist. They are the attributes of a good parent and a decent human being who has a fair degree of understanding of himself and his interpersonal relationships so that his own problems do not interfere, who is reasonably warm and empathic, not unduly hostile or destructive, and who has the talent, dedication and compassion to work co-operatively with others.

Counselling is an important form of human intervention in other people's lives. All such intervention is 'value-laden'. What must be ensured is that its value is positive and thus leads to creative growth.

REFERENCES

1. Ethel Venables, *Counselling*, National Marriage Guidance Council, 1973, p.8.
2. H.J. Eysenck, *The Effects of Psychotherapy*, in *Handbook of Abnormal Psychology*, Pitman Medical, 1960, pp.697–725
3. C.B. Truax & R.R. Carkhuff, *Towards Effective Counselling and Psychotherapy*, Chicago, Aldine, 1968
4. Una Maguire, *Counselling Effectiveness: a Critical Discussion*, British Journal of Guidance and Counselling, Jan 1973, p.43.
5. Maxim Gorki, 'Two Stories', *The Dial*, 1927, pp.197–8.
6. Bernard Martin, *Healing for You*, Lutterworth Press, p.131.
7. Eric Wood, 'The need to make judgments', *Contact*, No. 30, March 1970.
8. Samuel M. Natale, *British Journal of Guidance and Counselling*, July 1973, p.61.
9. Samuel M. Natale, op. cit. p.60.
10. Louis Marteau, *Ethical Standards in Counselling*, British Association for Counselling, Bedford Square Press of the National Council for Voluntary Organisations, 1974, pp.68–9.
11. Carl R. Rogers, *On Becoming a Person*, Constable, 1967, pp.39–58.

11   The Pastoral Dimension

The previous chapters of this book have been written from a neutral position as far as religion is concerned. This has been fully intentional, because we wanted to deal with counselling in general. Here and there we may have given ourselves away but, generally speaking, the foregoing should be as relevant to non-religious counsellors as to those functioning in the 'pastoral' areas. In point of fact, the word 'pastoral' is now sometimes used in secular settings, but in this final chapter we are giving it its original meaning.

Many coming for counselling do not realise they are looking for a workable philosophy of life. They just know themselves to be disturbed, and feel they are at the mercy of forces and factors beyond their control. They are looking for personal freedom, and protesting at the 'fated' feeling that oppresses them.

This quest for meaning has a religious feel about it. Everyone has lower and higher bits of experience and many do not know what to make of them, how to evaluate them. Marghanita Laski represents those who claiming to be atheists, still recognise they have religious needs.

Perhaps the churches have encapsulated the experience of many and crushed it into their own ritual systems and worship forms. People can be socialised into the use of ritual, but this can make insufficient allowance for an individual's private capacity. A great deal of formalised religion closes people down — and to that extent diminishes them — rather than opening them up, which is the task of counselling.

A well-known rabbi has said that his religious experience owed more to his analysis than to his pious Jewish upbringing, and in his broadcast on Jacky Gillott's suicide (already quoted), Gerald Priestland said it was not his religious exercises — he is a Quaker — but psychiatry and drugs that brought him relief from his depression.

It is sometimes said that our sense of otherness, of a reality beyond ourselves, has become impoverished. Monica Furlong writes: 'This is a society that represses transcendence. Learning to admit transcendence may be the major undertaking of a man's life. Ignore it, and the personality is stunted, or destroyed.'

Yet everyone does have an experience of otherness, which has religious value. Falling in love, making love and bringing a new life into the world, the actual experience of parenthood, the awareness of the beauty of nature — these are all experiences that put us in touch with a reality beyond our awareness of ourselves. We speak of 'falling in love' — the love is not created by the two people involved; it is there; it is given; the experience is 'between' and even 'beyond' them. So we go on to say, 'This thing (i.e. love) is bigger than both of us.' It is the contacting of another dimension. Even negative feelings can have a religious feel and value. The feeling of disappointment, of an emptiness within, suggests that there should be a fulness that is somehow lacking.

We are not suggesting that the counsellor should exploit any of these feelings that, in our view, have religious overtones. He stays within the client's terms of reference. Any suggestion that he should manipulate the client into a particular pattern of religious response would be a denial of all principles of good counselling. He wants the client to become as fully aware as possible of his own capacity to respond to the heights and depths of human experience. If he is moving towards selfhood, becoming more fully human, developing his capacity for self-awareness, affirming himself — these are all functions of a healthy religion.

In every meaningful relationship participants sense that there is more than what each contributes. Something extra is given. The history of religion — and here we are not thinking only of the Jewish and Christian faiths — centres very largely upon the two basic requirements of counselling, and psychotherapy. Firstly, the client feels the need for some protection from inner forces that are haunting him; and secondly, as this need is allayed, the therapist is still there offering a steady, mature relationship which the client can use to discover and develop his personal resources. It is the uniqueness of our personal life that is seeking satisfaction. To some extent this satisfaction happens in the best of counselling relationships, which is akin to what a creative religious experience also provides.

This is not to suggest that religion is a cure for all psychological and emotional ills, any more than it offers full physical health to its devotees. Harry Guntrip wrote:

> In some cases a religious experience stabilizes a profoundly disturbed person, as can be seen from the lives of such men as John Bunyan, George Fox, Jeremiah, and St. Paul. In other cases a person has to sustain his religious faith and experience in the face of continuing psychic disturbances as with the badly depressed Luther. In yet other cases, severe psychoneurosis adulterates religious experience, reducing it to exceedingly immature and neurotic forms.[1]

It is true that Freud saw religion as a great illusion, and therefore neurotic, but no one can be right all the time. Ever since Freud's heyday, post-Freudians have been correcting, modifying, and changing altogether a great deal of what he said and wrote. In any case, Carl Jung, who once was a disciple but found it necessary to go his own way, made a very different emphasis. We have already quoted his well-known statement that most of his clients who were in the second half of life needed to find some religious satisfaction before they could find emotional wellbeing. As President of the International Conference on Psychotherapy held at Oxford as far back as 1938, he answered the question as to whether religious experience is valid with an emphatic *yes*, and in his closing sentence averred that in so far as we are without it we are a little insane.

This brings us to consider the relationship between psychiatry (including all forms of psychotherapy) and religion. That they have a great deal in common cannot be doubted. They both deal with our inner world. Sometimes they even use the same technical language.

Words common to both psychiatry and religion include: guilt, forgiveness, responsibility, separation, reconciliation.

Words used in religion but not in psychiatry proper include: sin, worship, grace, salvation.

Words used in psychiatry but rarely or never in religion include: alienation, disintegration, therapy, transference.

The close examination of these groups of words makes it clear that though different language is sometimes used, we are describing and seeking to understand similar processes.

An important obligation that rests with the counsellor is the learning of his client's language. This means not simply noting the words he uses, but ensuring he knows what the words actually mean to the client. He will not assume that the client means precisely the same as he himself means by, say, such words as anxiety, depression, guilt. Should the client use religious words, these too need to be checked out, otherwise communication between them may suffer.

Perhaps it would help to take one of the words used in both psychotherapy and religion, and one theological word, in order to understand the nature of the overlap that obviously exists. First of all, let us take the various meanings of the word 'guilt' which has links with a whole range of other significant words, such as 'conscience', 'confession' and 'forgiveness'. Then we will examine the religious word 'sin'.

The first thing to be said about guilt is that there are many varieties, most of them false. We know of morbid guilt, unreal guilt, infantile guilt, pathological guilt. This does not mean there is no such thing as *real* guilt. With so many counterfeits there simply must be a true currency somewhere. The task of the client, helped by the therapist, is to determine what is *true* guilt, why it comes, what it means and how it needs to be resolved.

Morbid guilt comes from a negative conscience. In Kafka's novels (*The Trial, The Castle*) the hero has a conscience which arrests him before he has done anything wrong and sentences him without revealing what he has done. There are such people, and some of them find their way to the counsellor.

Freud explained our guilt feelings as being the result of social constraint. A child's parents scold him. This creates the fear that he will lose their love. This is sometimes called 'functional guilt', because it results from social suggestion, and the fear of consequences i.e. the loss of respect, etc.

Jung thought that guilt flows from the refusal to accept ourselves in a total way, in our resistance to integrate into consciousness the 'shadow' part of ourselves.

Buber went further than this. He saw that guilt turns on some violation of human relationships, and is a breach in the I-Thou relationship. Guilt involves others.

There is a 'value-guilt' which does not come from social constraint, but follows the betrayal of an authentic standard. It is a free judgment of the self by the self. There is such a thing as moral conviction.

People often use the word 'guilt' when they mean 'fear' or sometimes 'resentment'. The prohibitive or infantile conscience (i.e. the undeveloped conscience) diverts the attention from what has been done to the fear of consequences. It is more fear than guilt. Similarly when friends or relatives make unreasonable demands and we summon up courage to refuse, we say we have guilty feelings, but the basic feeling may be resentment at being put in the position of having to say *No*.

Others develop an 'authoritative' conscience. They must have the approval of authority — parents, teachers, employers, neighbours, the church. They feel they ought to obey authority, rather than ought to do the right. Totalitarian systems and institutions create and are then maintained by this kind of conscience.

The super-ego is sometimes called the unconscious conscience. From years nought to five, infants are introjecting the commands and standards of their parents and others, and thereafter imagine that the resulting standards and attitudes are their own when they are, in fact, 'borrowed'. The function of the ego is to form a conscious conscience, which operates from 'ought' and not 'must'; that acts on moral insight rather than childish prohibitions. We now keep ourselves clean not because we were made to bath as children, but because we have seen the hygienic value of bathing, and actually like to feel clean.

More than anything else, it is the concept of 'sin' that seems to infuriate the non-religious, but there is here a great deal of misunderstanding. Whatever is meant theologically by 'original sin', it presupposes something more fundamental still — an original righteousness from which the sin is a departure. Sin is a meaningless concept except for spiritual personalities. 'There is no sin in the farmyard', or the jungle. There may be sin in the farmer and in the explorer.

A Biblical definition of sin is a 'falling short' and this is something everyone knows in his experience of life. It is true that in the Bible it is a falling short 'of the glory of God', but even here it is speaking of man's greatness. Undoubtedly Christians have thought of sin too much in terms of man breaking God's laws, when essentially it is the repudiation of a filial relationship with God as Father. The Pharisees in the Gospels show that the keeping of rules can be sinful, to the extent that it does not foster growth. Obeying rules makes for a self-righteousness in which there is no awareness of guilt. The guilt then becomes unconscious and issues in projection. There is the well-known story of the Pharisees bringing to Jesus a woman taken in adultery, demanding that He should add His condemnation to theirs. This He refused to do but sought to turn the eyes of the Pharisees inwards, thus helping to make their own guilt conscious.

Sin may be defined as our failure to respond to love. Some non-religious therapists speak of an individual's 'defiant withdrawal', of his 'self-absorption', of his 'refusal of the love of others'. Is not the difference here, as elsewhere, very largely a question of a different vocabulary?

A dangerous tendency in some of today's thinking is to seek to exonerate man altogether from any responsibility for his actions. It is true that we do sometimes blame people when they are not responsible. There is such a condition as moral disease when actions are determined by compulsive forces, where the will is powerless. There is, however, a danger of explaining away all wrong actions. This inevitably leads to a diminution of personal responsibility, whereas counselling is concerned with enabling a person to accept more responsibility for his particular actions and total life.

All human actions and decisions cannot be laid at the door of heredity and environment. This would be to rob life of all meaning and dignity. To explain away evil would be to belittle man, for to excuse wrong is simply to embrace a new kind of determinism.

The non-religious counsellor may help his client come to terms with his 'moral failure complex'. The pastoral counsellor may be able to help his 'religious' client to see 'sin' and 'guilt' as the raw materials of a spiritual personality rather than as life's waste products.

Let us describe an actual client/counsellor encounter:

> Robert phoned the centre in a state of great agitation and when he arrived an hour later this had not abated. His first words were: 'If you're going to ram religion down my throat, I'll leave immediately.' He was reassured.
>
> He then described a breakdown in his relationship with his wife whom he dearly loved. The previous week he had lied to her for the first time. Not knowing how to bear the guilt of this, he was distraught for days.
>
> He had not been to church for years except to get married — but on the previous Sunday had gone into a nearby church, in between the services, and prayed for forgiveness. He felt no different and still had not confessed the lie to his wife.

This young man had said 'no religion', and yet had himself brought it into the counselling room. What he was really saying was, 'I feel sufficiently self-condemned. Please don't add your condemnation to mine.'

We will look at this counselling situation in the light of some of the words mentioned above. Robert experienced feelings of 'guilt' — a word used in both psychotherapy and religion. He was aware of having done 'wrong' — the religious person might here use the word 'sin'. He experienced 'alienation' from his wife — a word most frequently used in psychological circles. He went to church in order to 'confess' and find 'forgiveness'. Both religious words but in therapy the word 'confess' might give way to such a phrase as 'making a clean breast of it'. Later Robert did confess to his wife, and her 'forgiveness' banished his feeling of 'alienation'. This was an experience of 'reconciliation', a word used in both camps. The other religious word for this is 'atonement' — the divide had been bridged and once more they were 'at one'.

It can be seen that in religion and counselling we are in touch with the same dynamic realities. The fundamental difference, of course, lies in the religious person's belief in a transcendent, personal reality, i.e. God. The humanist will say, 'Why drag God in?' The Christian will reply, 'There is no need to, He's there already.' Jesus Christ shows that humanity is not alien to, or separate from, divinity. It can be its vehicle of expression. Discovering our human heights and depths is the discovering of God.

So while the pastoral counsellor will not take the religious initiative, he will be open to the spiritual, to the realm of ultimate meaning. He is interested in the fundamental questions regarding life and its meaning.

We believe that, all things being equal, a healthy religion will produce a healthy personality. If it produces neurosis and breakdown, then it is illusion. But all things are rarely equal and we are not saying that religion will automatically cure a neurosis or a depression, any more than it will cure diabetes. Our point is that it should not *create* the neurosis. There is a difference between Christian neurotics and neurotic Christians. A neurotic person can have a healthy faith, and a normal person can have a neurotic religion.

Unfortunately there is a great deal of unhealthy religion in existence. The doctor knows that his therapies are as dangerous as they are helpful. Proper quantities of a drug can bring health; overdoses can kill. Religion, too can be as dangerous as it can be helpful. It can hurt instead of heal. It can also be used for the purpose of self-deception, as a defence against reality, which is something of which Jesus and the prophets were acutely aware.

We are not suggesting that religion should be *used* as a means of allaying anxiety and comforting distressed people. The attempt to use prayer as a means of help is simply turning religion into another form of magic. The relief, the comfort, the strength that religion brings to many believers are the by-product of their relationship with God, and it is on that relationship the life of devotion is concentrated.

We must distinguish between religion as law and religion as grace. It is the religion of law that is inimical to inner wellbeing, because it generates fear rather than love. 'Musts' and 'must nots' can only lead to a restriction of life.

A group of religious believers were asked for the most frightening text in the Bible. Nearly all of them chose: 'Thou God seest me', which they interpreted as meaning that God was life's policeman, or Big Brother, when in fact it means something beautiful and comforting, i.e. that God in His loving concern for us *keeps us in view*. To quote Harry Guntrip once more:

Religion can be so taught as to emphasize and confirm the deep inner subordination and stifled spontaneity of the vital heart of the personality. It is a common experience in psychotherapy to find patients who fear and hate God, a God who, in the words of Professor J.S. Mackenzie, 'is always snooping after sinners', and who 'becomes an outsize of the threatening parent. That means almost irreparable damage. The child grows up fearing evil rather than loving good; afraid of vice rather than in love with virtue. To the degree the parents elicit guilt-feelings to that degree the child grows up with a feeling of insecurity'.[2]

The above quotation calls Isabel to mind:

She was in her late forties and came for counselling suffering from depression. Her early home background had been narrowly religious. She spoke of her father with fear. Now a married woman with two teenage daughters herself, her eighty year old father was continuing to dominate and frighten her, even though he lived some two hundred miles away.
A Sunday school chorus from her childhood was still resonating in her mind: 'My God is writing all the time'. She winced as she said the words. 'I see black marks against my name, nothing but black marks.' At times she had tried, without success to liberate herself from what she had come to see as a destructive religious upbringing. Her fear of her father had completely distorted her view of God. It took over three years for the picture to change, and even then the old fear intermittently returned.

An unhappy religion should be a contradiction in terms. Any seeking of suffering for its own sake, any despising of this lovely world, any negative attitude to the physical aspects of our human life, is neurotic. One of the most damaging of religious snares is that of perfectionism. This can make for self-deception on the one hand or dissatisfaction and misery on the other. Some religionists seem to go through life blaming earth for not being heaven. A sense of reality is an essential element in healthy religion.

At this point we would like to refer the reader back to the section in chapter 8 dealing with existential anxiety. Howard Clinebell states our predicament in this way:

> Anxiety in general is the response of the human organism to anything that is perceived as a threat to what one regards as essential to one's welfare or safety. Pathological (neurotic) anxiety arises when contradictory impulses, desires or need clamor simultaneously for expression or satisfaction. It is the result of inner conflict. It serves the function of keeping material that is unacceptable to the self-image repressed. In contrast, existential anxiety is nonpathological or normal anxiety. It arises from the very nature of human existence. Man is the animal who knows he will die. He is trapped by his rootage in nature. He is subject to its forces of sickness, pain, and death, and he lacks what Big Daddy, in Tennessee Williams' *Cat on a Hot Tin Roof,* calls the 'pig's advantage' — viz. ignorance of his mortality.[3]

Here we want to ask some fundamental questions: In what constructive way can the non-religious therapist deal with the existential anxiety of his client? Ordinary day to day anxiety is difficult enough to handle, but what of the basic terrorising concern regarding existence itself? Is there a psychological or psychotherapeutic answer to anxiety about one's right to exist?

The answer cannot be to encourage people to seek distraction and escape routes. Nor is it right to help people to be less than alive to their own pain, misgivings and uncertainties.

Some people's neuroses are in fact a protection against their existential anxiety. They lessen their aliveness, diverting their anxieties in the direction of the less important issues. Paul Tillich saw neurotic anxiety as a way of avoiding the threat of non-being by the unconscious evading of a full participation in life. It is a way of defending yourself from the fear of death by not being fully alive. To use T.S. Eliot's phrase, they are only 'partly living'.

What we are suggesting is that either there is no adequate psychotherapeutic answer to existential anxiety or there is a religious answer. To us there is something frightening about the atheistic denial of a greater personal reality than man. Is a man the measure of all things? Is he to be for ever alone except for his fellowman? Perhaps the present space-quest is in part motivated by the need to find other greater intelligences so that if man fails, others may still be able to succeed. Man is looking for a meaning beyond himself in which he can discover the significance of his individual reality.

An important part of life must be the attempt to make some sense of it. There are those who believe that psychotherapy in all its forms may become a symptom of the pathology of our day and age. If it is to remain truly therapeutic it needs a reasonably correct picture of man and a fair idea as to the meaning of man's life.

Our preference is to use the word 'spiritual' of man, but we have fallen into the way of using 'religious' because — as we have seen — even non-believers recognise they have religious needs. They may feel less comfortable with the words 'spirit' or 'spiritual'. And yet, transcendence is part of everyone's life. We can separate ourselves from our bodies, minds and emotions. There is a centre of consciousness that transcends these aspects of us.

Some years ago when theologians seemed to be trying to get rid of 'transcendence' it was such sociologists as Peter Berger[4] who brought the concept back into respectable usage.

Dr. Viktor Frankl, the internationally acclaimed Viennese psychiatrist wrote:

> Man lives in three dimensions: the somatic, the mental, and the spiritual. The spiritual dimension cannot be ignored, for it is what makes us human. To be concerned about the meaning of life is not necessarily a sign of disease or of neurosis. It may be; but then again, spiritual agony may have very little connection with a disease of the psyche. The proper diagnosis can be made only by someone who can see the spiritual side of man. Psychoanalysis speaks of the *pleasure principle*, individual psychology of *status* drive. The pleasure principle might be termed *the will-to-pleasure*; the status drive is equivalent to the *will-to-power*. But where do we hear of that which most deeply inspires man; where is the innate desire to give as much meaning as possible to one's life, to actualise as many values as possible — what I should like to call the *will-to-meaning*?[5]

We tend to think of physical, psychical and spiritual layers, but it might be better to think of body, mind and spirit as different dimensions of one and the same reality, so that our wholeness is not destroyed.

Albert Camus, the French existentialist and novelist, used to say that man must decide 'whether life deserves to be lived or not'.

We exist in order to discover, express and create meaning. One of the most important personal achievements in life is the developing of sound 'attitudinal values', to find the right way of reacting to what happens to us, and so being able to use every experience, including suffering. Mary Craig, describing how she came to terms and learned to live creatively with one son suffering from gargoylism and another from Down's Syndrome, says that the tragedy is not that we suffer but that we waste suffering. A character in a Walpole novel declares, 'It isn't life that matters but the courage you bring to it.'

There are elements in life that seem to be void of any meaning, and it is in these areas that a man can transcend himself. He can *give* meaning to life. Dross can be turned into gold, disaster into triumph. We question life, but life also questions us.

'Will I ever be the author of my life, or only its victim?' Life victimises everyone, some slightly, others beyond belief. Yet to go through life being a victim is to deny our essential nature. We can cease being victims. This is the message of healthy religion and good counselling.

Unless a man is insane, he has a measure of freedom, and that freedom can be extended. There is freedom in the face of instincts — man *has* instincts, they do not have him. There is freedom in the face of an inherited disposition — identical twins can build very different lives on the basis of identical predispositions. There is freedom in the face of a difficult environment — there can be two men in a concentration camp, one will degenerate, the other will survive gloriously.

This is not to pretend that life is easy, or that life is fair, because it is neither.

It is to affirm that in spite of all minimising factors, man decides for himself. 'We are our own choices'. The counsellor's task is to facilitate the client's ability to choose, to enlarge his capacity for making decisions, to clarify the vision of what life can mean.

POSTSCRIPT

How should we bring this book to its conclusion? In 1946 Herman Hesse was awarded the Nobel Prize for Literature for his great novel *The Glass Bead Game*. It is regarded by many as a 'major contribution to contemporary philosophic literature and has a powerful vision of universality, the inner unity of man's cultural ideals and his search for personal perfection and social responsibility.'

The Penguin Modern Classics Edition, (1972) of this novel concludes with three of Hesse's short stories. Here are some extracts from one of these entitled: 'The Father Confessor'.

Josephus Famulus, at the age of thirty-six sought the solitude and peace of the desert, and some years later troubled souls began seeking him out, and in doing so discovered comfort in making their confession. Josephus found he had a gift.

> It was the gift of listening. Whenever a brother from one of the hermitages, or a child of the world harried and troubled of soul, came to Josephus and told him of his deeds, sufferings, temptations, and missteps, related the story of his life, his struggles for goodness and his failures in the struggle, or spoke of loss, pain or sorrow, Joseph knew how to listen to him, to open his ears and his heart, to gather the man's sufferings and anxieties into himself and hold them, so that the penitent was sent away emptied and calmed. Slowly, over long years, this function had taken possession of him and made an instrument of him, an ear that people trusted.
> His virtues were patience, a receptive passivity, and great discretion.
> He did not lose patience when someone talked at great length while obviously concealing the main issue. Nor was he stern when someone charged himself with delusory and invented sins. All the complaints, confessions, charges and qualms of conscience that were brought to him seemed to pour into his ears like water into the desert sands. He seemed to pass no judgment upon them and to feel neither pity nor contempt for the person confessing. Nevertheless, or perhaps for that very reason, whatever was confessed to him seemed not to be spoken into the void, but to be transformed, alleviated and redeemed in the telling and being heard. Only rarely did he reply with a warning or admonition, even more rarely did he give advice, let alone any order. Such did not seem to be his function, and his callers apparently sensed that it was not. His function was to arouse confidence and to be receptive, to listen patiently and lovingly, helping the imperfectly formed confession to take shape, inviting all that was damned up or encrusted within each soul to flow and pour out. When it did, he received it and wrapped it in silence.

Once when on a journey he heard two men talking about himself:

'What kind of thing does he do, this Famulus of yours?' 'Oh, you just go to confess to him, and I suppose people wouldn't go if he wasn't good and didn't understand things. The story is he hardly says a word, doesn't scold or bawl anyone out, doesn't order penances or anything like that. He's supposed to be gentle and shy.'

'But if he doesn't scold and doesn't punish and doesn't open his mouth, what does he do?'

'They say he just listens and sighs marvellously and makes the sign of the cross'.

REFERENCES

1. Harry Guntrip, *Mental Pain and the Cure of Souls*, Independent Press, 1957, p.189.
2. Harry Guntrip, op. cit. p.194.
3. Howard J. Clinebell, Jnr., *Quarterly Journal of Studies on Alcohol*, Sept. 1963, p.477.
4. Peter L. Berger, *A Rumour of Angels*, Penguin Books, 1971.
5. Viktor L. Frankl, *The Doctor and the Soul*, Penguin Books, 1973, p.9.